M000198951

A HIGHER
ROAD

*Cleanse Your Consciousness to Transcend
the Ego and Ascend Spiritually*

by

D. NEIL ELLIOTT

*A Seven-Step Process to Inner Peace, Joy, Love,
Abundance, and Prosperity*

Copyright © 2021 by D. Neil Elliott
Published in Canada by Elliott & McAdam Productions
Published in the USA by Elliott & McAdam Productions

All rights reserved. No part of this book may be reproduced by any mechanical, photographic, or electronic process, or in the form of a phonographic recording; nor may it be stored in a retrieval system, transmitted, or otherwise be copied for public or private use—other than for "fair use" as brief quotations embodied in articles and reviews—without prior written permission of the publisher.

The author of this book does not dispense medical advice or prescribe the use of any technique as a form of treatment for physical, emotional, or medical problems without the advice of a physician, either directly or indirectly. The intent of the author is only to offer information of a general nature to help you in your quest for emotional, physical, and spiritual well-being. In the event you use any of the information in this book for yourself, the author and the publisher assume no responsibility for your actions.

To protect the privacy of others, certain names and details have been changed.

Library of Congress Cataloging-in-Publication Data

Elliott, D. Neil
A Higher Road. Cleanse Your Consciousness to Transcend the Ego and Ascend Spiritually.
/ D. Neil Elliott. – 1st ed.
p. cm.

Library of Congress Control Number: 2021909421

Paperback ISBN: 978-1-7777172-5-4
Hardcover ISBN: 978-1-7777172-4-7
eBook ISBN: 978-1-7777172-3-0
Audio ISBN: 978-1-7777172-0-9

This book is dedicated to my grandchildren, Bruce, Lydia, Hailey, Christiana, and Samantha.

<u>Love Is</u>

Love is soft
gentle
kind.
It embraces
enfolds
enshrines.
It is patient
understanding
sublime.
Love is all these things.
Let it shine.

— Received in Meditation
by D. Neil Elliott —

TABLE OF CONTENTS

PREFACE

This book introduces you to a number of key concepts designed to open your mind and help you consider new perspectives about life. The process outlined in the *Seven Steps* requires that you complete two additional readings. The first is a recommended book that shares its author's real-life experience—her story will stretch your concept of where we come from and where we return to after the death of our bodies. The final reading—required—is a vital *blueprint* document that will enable you to change the course of your life completely.

THE RECOMMENDED APPROACH TO READING THIS BOOK

To get the most out of this book, I recommend you read it from cover to cover so you can understand the process in its entirety. Then go back and do the required work, starting with Step One. Alternatively, if you are unfamiliar with the topics discussed in the science section, prior to starting Step One, you may begin by reading one or more of the suggested scientific readings first.

The cover-to-cover method of reading (prior to starting Step One) will prepare you (and your mind) for the detailed work required in each of the *Seven Steps* by introducing you to several high-level concepts that are crucial for you to understand before you embark on the seven-step process. The approach will help ensure that you learn the fundamental concepts in stages so you can build upon them and lay a solid foundation for wholesale change. Are you ready to create a brand-new, vibrant, and empowered you? Let's get started....

INTRODUCTION

I wrote this book to share the new knowledge, process, and methodology I learned to transform my consciousness to one of Love, Peace, Joy, and Abundance. My hope is that this information will help those who desire to transform their individual consciousness to experience for themselves an ever more exalted and wondrous state of living. Our individual transformations in consciousness will gain momentum and eventually, we will change the behavior of humankind (the collective). When this happens, we will save our planet from human-driven annihilation. This may take many centuries, but it starts today with readers like you—readers open to learning, willing to transform their lives, and motivated to becoming the embodiment of Unconditional Love.

ACKNOWLEDGEMENTS

This book would not have been written without unconditional support and encouragement from my lovely wife, Marion (a.k.a. "Elizabeth" in the book). My gratitude is eternal.

Special thanks go out to my friends, Wasi and Sabbir, for their ongoing encouragement to complete this project.

Sincere thanks to all of my beta readers, Linda, Arlene, Renee, and Marion, who provided insightful comments and suggestions and identified small and important anomalies. Their support and feedback improved the end product and readability of this manuscript.

Heartfelt thanks also to my editor, Michael K. Ireland, whose edits I was grateful to accept, over and over, because they were so on point. She just made this book better!

Gratitude to the entire team at PRESStinely; in particular, Kristen Wise, Maira Pedreira and Zora Knauf for shepherding this book through the publishing gates! Your support is felt and so appreciated.

Finally, thanks to all the readers who have taken up my challenge to follow the practices outlined in this book—together, we are walking A Higher Road.

—D. Neil Elliott

NOTE TO READER

The names of all persons mentioned in this book (except for Rob and Gretchen Beach) have been changed to protect the innocent, to shield the irascible, and to respect those who wish to remain anonymous.

Note also that when quoting from the "Letters," I have removed most of the original special formatting (e.g., centering, italics, bold print, underlining, etc.) to create an easier reading experience for you and to optimize text flow within this, my book. If you would like to read the text in its original format, I have provided a link to an online source in Chapter 7.

Except where noted, all online citation information was accessed May 7 – 28, 2021.

PART I

THE ROAD NOT TAKEN

Two roads diverged in a wood, and I—
I took the one less traveled by,
And that has made all the difference. [1]

—Robert Frost

Chapter 1

THE FORK IN MY ROAD

We must make the choices that enable us to fulfill the deepest capacities of our real selves.[2]

—Thomas Merton

Two days after Elizabeth flew to Toronto to visit family and friends, I sat down at the kitchen table in our one-bedroom apartment and crafted my suicide note. Fifty-seven years old, I was deeply depressed, full of angst and anxiety, and stricken by fears and phobias. I felt like I was trapped in a cage. My life was an abyss of sadness, sorrow, and self-pity—I saw no way out. I needed time to say goodbye to my loved ones without them realizing what I planned to do.

I am a professional engineer with an MBA. I had been contemplating this final act for a few weeks, planning an orderly exit, so as not to leave my wife, Elizabeth, stranded financially. Soon, our crippling mortgage debt would be cleared: After having been listed for six years, finally, our house had sold. The housing market had crashed in late 2007 and in our area, it had not recovered. We had lost a substantial sum of our savings, but my life insurance would secure Elizabeth's financial future.

I had recently read Anita Moorjani's bestselling book, *Dying to Be Me*. After four long years of suffering from an increasingly aggressive cancer, Anita had lapsed into a coma on the way to the hospital. After assessing her in Emergency, the attending physician informed Anita's husband that she would not make it through the night. But after twenty-four hours, Anita came out of her coma, sat up, and declared that she would be okay. Within days, she recovered, and after two weeks the medical team could not find a trace of cancer in her body.

In her book, Anita describes the remarkable, vivid near-death experience (NDE) she'd had while she was in the coma. She wrote her book to share with the world the messages she had received "on the other side." We are neither judged nor punished for what we do here on Earth, Anita explained. *Even if we commit suicide?* I wondered. What she said was believable (albeit not understandable).

But Anita's book helped to alleviate a nagging, Christian-based fear in the back of my mind: *What would happen to me if I committed suicide?* I felt I had permission to escape the pain, the depression, and the treadmill that bore me ever further into despair and hopelessness. In other words, her book gave me permission to end my life.

Coincidentally, I had just come across a new manuscript that gave me a glimmer of hope. This document reveals facts concerning human existence and the spiritual origins of personality. These spiritual truths take time to study, practice, and absorb. The manuscript's purpose is to enable humanity to construct a new consciousness during this new millennium. It contains the seeds of our future spiritual evolution. It is this consciousness evolution that brings about the mental and physical evolution in our personal lives, and when collectively each of us is evolved, we will bring humanity into a state of peace and harmonious wellbeing. I felt drawn to study that "one last set of Truths," as the author promised that knowing them would liberate me. Suicide was always an option, but deep down it felt wrong—so I gave life one last chance. I set a timeline (the engineer and project manager in me needed a schedule) and began to study.

This set of Truths is rational and believable. Each Truth bridges the gulf between science and spirituality. Each is in alignment with (and indeed goes well beyond) the information and messages Anita Moorjani brought back from her NDE. Collectively, these Truths helped me to understand the origins of life and existence and gave me enough hope that to this day, I continue to study, absorb, and practice them consistently. They turned my depression, hopelessness, and despair into peace, joy, and love—and changed my life. These Truths are for everyone (agnostic or atheist) and they transcend all religious differences (the beliefs of Christianity, Islam, Buddhism, Hinduism, Sufism, Judaism...), citizenship or ethnic identity (Israeli, Palestinian, Australian, Canadian, German, Japanese...), as well as any other spiritual beliefs or philosophical views.

In this book, I share these Truths with you so that you too will have knowledge that will enable you—with effort, determination, and dedication—to transform your life. Regardless of your current situation and challenges, whether they are physical or mental; whether you are poor or wealthy; and whether you are ill or healthy, happy or depressed, the steps and information provided can help you along your path to a brighter, more fulfilling future. This book brings together scientific discoveries and spiritual truths that explain the Truth of our Existence in a factual, rational, and engaging way. It outlines clearly how you can achieve your life's purpose, heal your body and mind, and draw happiness and peace into your life. The seven-step process presented can guide you into a life of peace, joy, love, abundance, and prosperity.

This book has five Parts. Part I, the overview, is an introduction to the book and its contents. Part II is a recap of my history and experiences. It explains how and why I ended up at that kitchen table, penning a suicide note. More importantly, it illustrates how I used my creative consciousness tools (albeit unknowingly and ignorantly) to construct both my future and my day-to-day life experiences—both good ones I enjoyed and bad ones I merely endured. You will understand how I did this (and how to do it for yourself) once you have completed all seven steps outlined in this book.

Part III presents scientific discoveries that will open your mind so you can comprehend the Truths shared in Part IV. Part III ends with a glimpse, a sliver of a vision—of the Truth of our reality (the place whence we came and to which we will return). This vision is drawn from Anita Moorjani's vivid account of her personal NDE experience and is shared with you to help you expand your current thinking and enable you to imagine more clearly the Truth of your reality.

Part IV explains the process of creation and human existence and reveals the Truth about your reality. It describes clearly that you are a creative being, using the creative tools of consciousness (unknowingly) to create every experience and circumstance that comes into your life. You will continue to use these tools of consciousness unknowingly until you understand these Truths. Provided within is the knowledge and the process for you to learn how to use these tools deliberately to attain absolute peace, joy, love, and abundance and to discover your true purpose in life. You cannot escape the process of consciousness. The tools of creativity are exact and undeviating, infinite, and eternal.

Part IV also outlines the reasons we behave as we do and why the world is in such a shocking state of upheaval and misery. It explains how each of us individually can transform our lives to be in absolute alignment with that *heavenly state* from which our souls were born and took their individuality. It reveals how to gain control of your life and change it for the better.

Part V documents personal insights and experiences that resulted after I followed the process and did the work laid out in this book.

The concluding chapter offers my thoughts on how you can best use all of this information and this process so you can achieve your true purpose in life. This process truly can bring you peace of mind. It can initiate, for you, a spiritual spiral of ever more exalted and wondrous living. I can make this last statement because one year after starting this process, I experienced the state of rapturous and joyous unconditional love that Anita Moorjani vividly describes having experienced during her NDE.

None of this information comes from me. I am merely an instrument, sharing these Truths and new knowledge, helping to guide you through the process to the best possible outcome. If you complete all *Seven Steps* as outlined, you will have the best chance of digesting and understanding these Truths and new knowledge. Please do all the Steps in order. If you are dedicated, determined, and patient, there is no simpler way to transform your life.

I realize, of course, that some readers may not be as fascinated with my history as I am. In that case, feel free to jump directly to Part III and begin the process of opening your mind to this unique wisdom. You will, however, be missing out on how my life experience demonstrates how each of us creates our every tomorrow.

I am glad you are joining me on this journey along A Higher Road.

PART II

MY HISTORY AND THE PATH TO SUICIDE

*Progress is impossible without change,
and those who cannot change their minds
cannot change anything.* [3]

—George Bernard Shaw

Chapter 2

CHILDHOOD

The best and most beautiful things in the world cannot
be seen or even touched; they must be felt with the heart.[4]

—Helen Keller

I was born in May 1960 and grew up in a small beach community, about twenty miles south of Vancouver, British Columbia (B.C.). A summer resort area, Boundary Bay was predominantly a community of beach houses—about 50 percent permanent residents and the rest temporary summer visitors. I was the youngest of six children; I have four older sisters and an older brother. The lineup is: Debbie, Mary, Abby, Randy, Rita, and me. There were roughly two years between each child. Debbie is twelve years my senior; Rita is three years older than me.

Our family lived with our black Labrador retriever, Luke, in a home with seven bedrooms and two bathrooms. Once a small, war-era, two-bedroom, one-bath, single-level home, my parents added to it in 1960. The expansion was a nine-hundred-square-foot, two-level box with a common wall between the original house and the new addition. The main level of the new structure had a large kitchen, a dining room, and a living room with a wood-burning fireplace. The upper level had five bedrooms and one bathroom. The house sat on three-quarters of an acre of flat land; a four-car garage was separate from the house and bordered the rear lot line. The design of the addition, being a complete house in its own right, ended up being extremely useful in generating additional income in future years. With the addition of a few locks on a few doors, the small bungalow portion could be rented out as a one- or two-bedroom home.

Our community had a two-room, two-teacher elementary school, aptly named "Boundary Beach Elementary," for grades one to four. After grade four, students took a bus for two and a half miles to the Boundary Bay Elementary school in Tsawwassen, a suburban community in southwest Delta that calls itself "the sunniest place in Metro Vancouver." Boundary Bay Elementary (not to be confused with Boundary Beach Elementary) taught grades one through seven. Tsawwassen Junior Secondary taught grades eight and nine, and South Delta Senior Secondary (SDSS), built in 1973, housed grades ten through twelve.

My dad worked as a machinist for the local government-owned-and-operated BC Ferries Corporation, a ferry system that connects the mainland with Vancouver Island and other Gulf Islands. Mom had an undergraduate university degree in home economics and on graduation taught for one year at the Jericho High School for the visually and hearing impaired. Then she and my dad got married, started a family, and her focus changed to a stay-at-home mom and family caregiver. With six kids, that was a full-time job.

Mom and Dad were both outdoorsy types. They liked to hunt ducks and pheasants in local farmers' fields; camp and canoe in remote areas of B.C., and enjoyed saltwater fishing in

Boundary Bay. Our parents were not affectionate towards their children, and compliments were scarce, but we could always count on having clean clothes, good food, and a home. They did not encourage us to have conversations with them, nor did they discuss matters with us.

We had happy and fun times together as a family, especially when Dad was with us and we went places, like going for picnics at the beach or going camping or fishing. Abby tells me that Dad played games or cards with the older children regularly on Sunday nights. Sometimes Mom joined in. Dad loved to joke and tease; Mom was more serious. She did laugh with her friends but not so much with her children.

Mom was a typical stay-at-home parent who took care of the children, did the laundry, cooked good meals, and baked homemade bread and goodies. When we became ill, she was great at nursing us back to health. Mom often helped out the elderly in the neighborhood and brought them homemade treats. However, all the kind things she did were overshadowed by unpredictable mood swings and violent rages. Her erratic behavior caused fear, anxiety, and stress in her children. The rages never happened when Dad was at home, so this was *safe time* for us. Then everything changed.

Saturday, July 3, 1965 was a warm, sunny summer day. My parents had been busy all day, and early that evening we sat down for an informal family dinner. Dad had not been feeling well and had a severe headache. But he had promised that before dinner he would set up a canvas tent in our backyard so that the four youngest of us six children could have a bit of fun camping that night. He kept his promise.

The oldest camper, Abby, was in charge. We settled in for an exciting night of sleeping outdoors. Mom and Dad slept (I thought) comfortably in their bed. But that night, Dad's headache escalated to the level of an extreme migraine, so Mom drove him (unbeknownst to me) to the local hospital, twenty miles away. The attending physician told him there was nothing he could do and prescribed aspirin and bed rest. They came home and went back to bed.

Early the next morning, Dad died. The autopsy concluded that the cause of death was a cerebral hemorrhage. Dad was forty-two years old and although he had worked for a branch of the provincial government, he had no life insurance. Mom was left with six kids, no job, and no income.

I vaguely remember having seen flashing lights and hearing voices through the tent walls in the early hours that Sunday morning. I woke later to an empty tent, unzipped myself from the sleeping bag, and ventured into the house. Two of my sisters were downstairs, crying. "What's wrong?" I asked.

"Go upstairs and ask Mom," they said.

Mom was sitting on the lid of the laundry hamper in the hall entrance, sobbing. "What's wrong, Mom?" I asked.

"Your dad died," she replied. Having just turned five, I did not really comprehend what that meant. I remember thinking, "Great, he won't spank me anymore," and was happy about that. Dad had large hands, and when he spanked me, it hurt. (Later in life, I found out that he had only spanked me once or twice, one swat each time—but my five-year-old brain had somehow connected a recent swat with relief that I wouldn't experience that again.)

About a week after Dad's death, I asked Mom, "When will Dad be coming home?"

"He won't ever be coming home," she said.

That's when Dad's death finally sunk in. I was truly sad ... for as long as a five-year-old stays sad ... not that long.

What follows here is a story of how my life—and how the lives of everyone in our family—unfolded after the death of our dad. Mom kept it together and raised her children as best she could as a single mom in the 1960s ... but it wasn't easy. As a result, our lives were a big adventure ... and not always a good one. Many of the fundamental beliefs, opinions, and thinking that brought me to that kitchen table on that fateful day were formed in the years of my childhood after we lost Dad. To this day, I wonder: *If Dad had not died, how might life have been different?* So, this is a synopsis of the story of my life and a recounting of incidents that shaped who I became and how I ended up, pen in hand, at that kitchen table at fifty-seven.

My personal history is provided here as an illustration of how my thinking, attitudes, and viewpoints about life shaped my verbal responses and emotional reactions to others, and to life in general. In short, I now realize that through my own beliefs and actions, I had driven myself to that kitchen table. The events that happened are not really important—they are merely a good example of how I created my future. They underpin what you will learn by reading this book. Although you may not understand fully the mechanisms presented (and while the stories I share may seem disparate at times), once you have completed this book, you will be able to connect the dots. Then you will be able to review your unique history and connect your own dots as well.

Before Dad died, we were an average family, probably no more dysfunctional than most large families who lived with a parent with uncontrollable rage. At the time of my dad's death, the emotional and financial strain on Mom—and on our whole family—was lost on me; I was only five.

As noted, I can trace many of my personal issues to disparate memories of my childhood and my interactions with my mother, brother, and sisters. While I no longer judge events or circumstances that happened in my childhood with disdain, condemnation, animosity, or blame, I can see now how the seeds of anxiety were planted in me because of who I was, how I saw my place in the world, and how those perceptions affected my decisions and behaviors. For example, one of my key personality challenges—a propensity toward chemical phobia—was born when I was very young.

As a machinist, my father had all the tools of his trade in a fully equipped workshop in our large garage. Against one wall was a metal lathe, an electric arc welder, a large drill press, and on and on. In another section at the back of the garage, on an island, was a wood lathe and other tools, and against the back wall were storage cabinets and a counter with a vice and other tools. On the floor, there was a twenty-four-inch-diameter, steel barrel about thirty-six inches long, cut in half vertically and laid end to end in a metal frame that Dad had built. This long, open barrel was filled partially with Varsol, a petroleum-based distillate and mineral spirit used for degreasing metal parts. At some point when I was between the ages of four and six, my mom scared the bejesus out of me by telling me, "Never go near these barrels or play with the contents. It will kill you." She meant well, but I took that threat seriously and to heart. I can see now that I planted this belief as a seed in my subconscious mind. The seed grew slowly in the form of fear and anxiety— and eventually into a phobia about dangerous chemicals. This eventually morphed into fears of commonly used chemicals such as paint thinner, antifreeze, and windshield washer fluid.

Somewhere between the ages of six and eight, I overheard a conversation Mom was having with some friends. She related a warning: "Never use a towel someone else has used. If they have a contagious disease and it's something medicine cannot deal with, you will be stuck with it for life." Again, I took the warning seriously ... as a threat to my safety and wellbeing. Another fearful belief was planted firmly in my subconscious mind. Again, the seed grew slowly: fear ... anxiety ... phobia. I was ever-vigilant: *Was anyone around me displaying what could be a viral disease that medicines could not treat?* By my twenties, the fear was so strong

I would avoid being in contact with (or even in the proximity of) such people. At work and in public, I was constantly on the lookout, identifying and avoiding people I perceived as displaying a possibly contagious viral disease. It consumed my thinking and was both mentally and physically exhausting.

Mom's well-intended admonitions had unintended consequences—they instilled in me, because of my personality type, several behaviors and phobias that (as it turned out) shaped my thinking; my emotional reactions to events, people, and circumstances; and the way my life unfolded.

So, there we were, in July 1965, our family grieving the loss of our father. Mom didn't have time to grieve, however; she had six mouths to feed. So, she buried Dad, and two weeks later, she started a summer school teaching program. Her undergraduate degree from the University of British Columbia enabled her to be accepted into a three-year summer school program to earn a teaching certificate. In addition, her undergraduate degree enabled her to secure a teaching position without possessing a teaching certificate. Therefore, she was able to obtain a job as a teacher at a high school about thirty miles from our home. She dedicated the next thirty years of her life to that career. She was our mom and our dad, the breadwinner and the homemaker, all rolled into one. She was a force of nature. Physically strong, strong-willed, independent, authoritarian, and temperamental, she could use a hammer and saw with the best of them ... as well as operate a sewing machine and a food mixer. She did her best to create good childhoods for us, and when things were good, the good stuff ranged from good to great. However, Mom had a dark side that overshadowed many of the good times and that shaped each of her children's behavior and responses to life. This dark side was exacerbated by Dad's death and the increased responsibilities Mom now had. In these dark moments, it was every kid for themselves.

Mom ruled with a *"my way or the highway"* attitude. She believed that if you *spare the rod, you spoil the child* and that *children should be seen and not heard.* Although I cannot speak for my siblings, for me, her intolerances, rages, and outbursts of verbal and physical abuse fueled selfish ego behaviors such as blaming, lying, and being defiant. I had not learned any other way to get my needs met or attain what I wanted or needed. She did not talk with us. She mostly talked *at us* with orders. I believe all of us were in survival mode. No one wanted to be subject to Mom's wrath. So, if I made a mistake or broke something, I lied, denied, or blamed the closest sibling.

Mom was liberal with her belief in discipline, and with me, she did not *spare the rod.* In the springtime of grade four, for example, I came home after school, checked in with my grandmother, and told her I was going out to play. I had hidden my bathing suit in our front door mailbox, so I could grab it as I left. My friend and I went down to the beach, something I was not supposed to do without an adult present. We went to play in the pools of water between the sandbars. When the tide went out, the sandbars and shallow pools in between them stretched out into the bay for about a mile. The pools ranged in depth from a few inches to two feet. We played in the warm water, looked for crabs, small shellfish, or geoducks.[5] We played for about an hour, then headed home so I could be home by curfew at 5:00 p.m.

The dirt path home from the beach ran beside our Grandma Rose's house and connected the two parallel streets we had to cross to get to the ocean. (Grandma Rose was my maternal grandmother, and she was a big part of my life.) As we were walking home, Mom pulled up in her car at the end of the path just up from Grandma's house. I waved and yelled, "Hi!" and ran with a big grin on my face to greet her. Grandma Rose was sitting in the front passenger seat. When I got to the car, Mom got out, holding a large carpet brush in her hand. It had a heavy, twelve-inch-long wooden handle. She grabbed me by the arm, and right there in front of my friend, while yelling at me for going to the beach without permission, she beat my backside with vicious and vigorous swings. When she pushed me into the back seat of the car, I hid on the floor, too ashamed to look at my friend. My bum hurt, but not as much as my pride. The outcome of this event (and others like it) stoked a reactionary, defiant response to authority. It also fueled my need to control my environment, to always know what lay ahead before I arrived, and to be cautionary about circumstances where I had to rely on someone else to escape (for example, leaving a party in a friend's car, on their timing). I was both humiliated and terrified.

Mom's rage terrorized me—and my impression is that we were all afraid of her. When I was nine years old, my sister Mary, her husband, and their firstborn child were renting the smaller part of the house. Rita, twelve, was visiting Mary and was sitting in the kitchen area of the unit. I do not remember why this happened, but I remember coming home and being beaten immediately with a leather belt for something I had done. I was backed into a corner, and Mom, wild with rage, was yelling and strapping me wherever she could hit bare skin. I was wearing a short-sleeved shirt, so my arms and torso were her target. I remember doing my best to protect my face from the onslaught. Rita told me recently that she and Mary wondered when the beating would stop. They were too afraid to intervene.

Looking back, I know now that Dad's demise created an overwhelming amount of pressure and stress for Mom that exacerbated her need to control her environment and her children's behavior. She was grieving, fearful, and angry. I was witness to outbursts of frustration, anger, and verbal and physical rage, sometimes directed at me, but mostly at my older siblings. But, while Mom could be violent and was never short on opinions about how things should or could be done, she could also, to me at least, be tender, generous, loving, and supportive. I have a few memories of her joy, humor, and uproarious laughter, but as I mentioned earlier, this was mostly with other adults, not her children. Now her new reality required her to get a job to support her family, and to figure out how to run a household of six kids while working and commuting for nine to ten hours a day, five days a week.

So, Mom is to be commended for having risen to all the challenges life set before her. As a matter of fact, I grew up with firsthand experience that when it comes to life or work, there is no difference between men and women. Mom just went out and got a good job. She would say, "If you want it, go get it." When I entered the workforce as a professional engineer, this belief prevented me from truly understanding the systemic barriers women experience in the workforce. My mom may have experienced them, but she never talked about them; she just went and did it. Upon reflection, that was quite an accomplishment, and one that she should be lauded for.

Our family survived the loss of my dad, and in some ways, we flourished. In other ways ... well ... to say it was "challenging" would be an understatement. Don't get me wrong. There was lots of good stuff in my childhood; we were not deprived. Both my parents grew up during the Great Depression; they had learned to be thrifty with their money. Mom and Dad did not have a mortgage, a line of credit or credit cards, or any debts. They only purchased things with cash and had no problem with delayed gratification. They built the addition to our house with their own hands—Mom often told us stories of collecting, straightening, and reusing bent nails. They wasted nothing. So, when Dad died without life insurance, Mom had a few savings to draw on to bridge us until her first pay at her new job, but that was all. Her frugality and her no-nonsense, get-it-done attitude enabled her to make the best of the situation and keep the family together.

Mom was grateful to have a job and a career, but work wasn't always great for her. She told stories constantly about her bosses and the insanity of "the system" in which she worked. She felt she had to fight continually for what was right, or for what she needed to teach her students properly. I remember thinking, "Wow, work is hard, and one has to put up with a lot of grief and stupid bosses."

I remember a conversation Mom was having with Grandma Rose, relating a story of someone who had won a million dollars. In 1968, that was enough money to set someone up for life. Mom talked about how wonderful life would be, to not have to work or worry about money, to do what you want, when you want, and to live a life of leisure. I latched onto this immediately. It was in stark contrast to her description of work. I thought about it, dreamed about it, and planted yet another seed that would grow to bear fruit in the future. That seed manifested into a driving purpose to make a lot of money. It did not matter what I did, as long as it was lawful and moral. My goal was to be rich as quickly as possible. This focus on wealth for the sake of wealth, without a drive or purpose to help society or others, proved to be a fool's errand that created dire consequences in my life. Another lesson for me to learn.

Again, don't get me wrong. I didn't develop a drive to be rich because we were poor. We weren't; we always had enough, and Mom did her best. For my entire childhood, we had plenty of food, a black-and-white television, and plenty of toys. I had lots of hand-me-downs in terms of toys and bicycles, but I always received new toys at Christmas or on my birthday. We all did. Of course, we didn't get everything we wanted, but what child does, or should? We had plenty.

Mom had a strong desire for me to get a university education. She encouraged me to make good grades and finish high school and promised that if I followed her rules, she'd pay for my university. If I didn't follow her rules, all bets were off. Through personal and individual circumstances for each of us,

I was the first of our brood to graduate with a university degree. I was grateful for Mom's financial help and support in making that happen.

I am so grateful to our mom for being so courageous in the face of adversity. After Dad died and Mom went to summer school, Grandma Rose looked after us for the summer. For the rest of the year, when my siblings went to school, she looked after me. A former teacher, Grandma Rose taught me to read and print, and when I started grade one in September 1966, I was ahead of the game.

As I noted earlier, from grades one to four, I attended Boundary Beach Elementary, two blocks from home. I walked or rode my bike to school. After school, I returned home to tea, cookies, and games or school lessons with Grandma Rose, who came to our house every day. My sisters and brother, who were bussed to and from various schools, arrived home at different times, between 3:30 p.m. and 4:30 p.m. Mom didn't get home until between 5:00 p.m. and 6:00 p.m., so my oldest sisters prepared our dinners and performed other household chores.

Being the youngest, I didn't have as much responsibility as my siblings, and as I grew up, I had increasing amounts of autonomy. In my first year of elementary school, Rita and I walked to school together. In grade two, since all of my siblings were at different schools and Mom left super early to drive to work, I got myself to school. In grade three, I was allowed to venture out into the neighborhood on my own to play with friends. We played "kick the can," "hide and seek," unorganized softball, and various other games.

I started playing organized softball on a team whose home base was our local elementary school baseball diamond. I played pitcher for four years on that team, and we won four championships. Mom attended one, perhaps two games over that entire time. I played two seasons of football, and Mom or one of my sister's boyfriends dropped me off and picked me up from practice or games. Neither Mom nor my siblings attended any of my practices or games. This did not make me feel neglected; it was just a part of my life. I thought it odd that parents of other kids had the time to attend practices or games to watch their kids play. This "life circumstance" likely fed into my attitude and independence that developed more fully in my early teen years.

In the fall of 1972, I played hockey. Practice and game times started at 4:30 a.m. or 5:00 a.m. Since Mom was working, I did not get to attend any practices during the week, and typically only attended games that landed on a Saturday or Sunday. It was an odd situation for my teammates and me. I did not know at the time that there were practices—Mom never told me. I thought we only played on game days and never gave it a second thought (although I noticed that while my teammates seemed pretty chummy, I did not know anyone).

Even though I played a lot of sports, I was a chubby child and my sisters teased me relentlessly. They would chant, "Fatty, fatty, two-by-four, couldn't fit through the bathroom door, so he did it on the floor...." I became so self-conscious of my weight that when I sat anywhere, other than at the table, I would try to hide my belly with a pillow.

In grade five, Mom put me on various diets; Metrecal diet drink (now considered a "1960's horror food") being one. My school lunches consisted of a few carrots, some celery sticks, and a can of chocolate Metrecal. None of the diets worked. I ended up having severe stomach pains, and the family physician concluded that I had the beginnings of a stomach ulcer. That resulted in another, even more restrictive diet. I think now that the physician misdiagnosed the issue: *A ten-year-old with a stomach ulcer?* Makes me pause. Anyway, by the age of thirteen, as I grew taller, my weight dropped off. I became a lanky teenager, but still I believed I was overweight. Any ounce of fat on my midsection brought shame and embarrassment—I imagined that everyone saw me the way I saw myself, and I perceived most attention as negative attention.

I did like being the center of good attention though; I liked to be center stage, in the spotlight. I liked to laugh, hear jokes, and tell jokes. I worked to make people laugh by being silly or saying something funny. When I was eight or nine, I participated in a community production as a clown. Mom designed and sewed the outfit, a colorful clown costume with a ruffled collar reminiscent of a clown in the Barnum & Bailey Circus. The production manager helped with my lines and jokes. I was a hit! I loved the applause and accolades. Another seed was planted, nurtured until ripe for harvest. To this day, I have a quirky sense of humor. Other people don't get many of my jokes, and I see some things as funny that others "just don't get." I will laugh at the weirdness of situations or happenings, and others just go "Huh?" Laughter is good for the soul ... so, look for the funny ... you will be surprised where and when you see it.

Unfortunately, as I grew into adulthood, I possessed no filter. A joke was a joke, regardless of the content. A colorful joke or not, if it made people laugh, it was good. I told jokes with no intent of malice, denigration, or ill will; I did not realize or understand why others could be offended by a joke's content or its insinuations—it was a joke. It was funny. This belief and lack of sensitivity for the feelings of others got me into trouble with a few female colleagues in my twenties. Eventually, I learned. In my thirties, I developed a filter.

I think my peculiar sense of humor was derived strictly from wanting to be noticed and liked. As the youngest of six, attention from other adults was limited. Their attention was focused mainly on adult things and teenagers' behavior. Mom had a sense of humor, but so did the rest of my siblings. None of them vied for attention by using humor (at least as far as I know).

But it's not that my humorous side made me an outcast ... and it's not that I didn't get any attention at all from my mom and my siblings. When things were good, we were "one big happy family." For example, since Mom taught home economics at a high school, we all had the same vacation days every year, and vacation time was family time. Each Christmas, Mom would buy copious quantities of food, make cakes and pies and other goodies, and she would ensure that we each received a variety of gifts and a stocking under the tree. We always had a huge Christmas feast with plenty of guests. It was a fun and joyous time. Every Easter and Thanksgiving we'd have another feast with family and guests—always a large turkey or ham and many vegetables, cakes, pies, cookies, and other delectable treats.

Every summer vacation, we got together and cleaned up our yard, the garage, and the house. Once that work was done, usually we went on an extended road trip, camping in provincial parks or campgrounds, and every second or third night staying in a motel to take a shower.

In the summer of 1967, Mom took Abby, Randy, Rita, and me on a six-week road trip through various routes in B.C., Alberta, the Northwest Territories, the Yukon, and Alaska. We saw the construction of the W.A.C. Bennett Dam, the largest earth-filled dam in B.C. We visited Dawson City in the Yukon and Anchorage in Alaska. We camped beside a remote river and enjoyed a bottle of champagne while watching the northern lights. (Well, okay, I was seven and had only a sip or two of champagne.) The Alaska Highway was constantly under construction and refurbishment, and many stretches of the road were so muddy that cars and trucks were towed through the muck and mire for miles by large Caterpillar bulldozers run by the construction crews. It was an adventure.

Many summers, we camped for two weeks in mid-August, beside Chezacut Lake in the Chilcotin district of B.C. We stood on the shore of the river and fished for returning-to-spawn Chinook salmon or rainbow trout. We canoed the lake while trolling for rainbow trout. We always returned home in time to attend the Pacific National Exhibition (P.N.E.) in Vancouver.

The fair ran for two weeks before Labor Day. The P.N.E. has a wooden roller coaster that was built in 1958 with 2,840 feet of track and reaches up to forty-five miles per hour on the steepest drop. It is historic, spectacular, and wonderfully fun to ride.

It is great to look back on the fun times we had on those family adventures. Sometimes, the memories of the good times overshadow the difficulties we all endured. Of course, all good things must end. Over time, as we all grew into adulthood, our family began to decline. The breaking up of our family began when Mom told both Debbie (age nineteen) and Mary (age seventeen), "Either follow my rules or get out before sundown." Debbie called her boyfriend immediately. He came a couple hours later to help her move out. Mary walked up the street to the family she babysat for regularly and told them. When she came home, she packed a bag and moved in with them. Both Debbie and Mary were married to their respective boyfriends within a few months.

Our third oldest sister, Abby (then sixteen), was hanging out with some "undesirables" (in Mom's estimation). Mom asked me routinely to spy on her. I was to report back to her on Abby's activities whenever her boyfriend came over. She would ask me to watch Abby's date's car through one of the upstairs bedroom windows. Typically, the car was parked out by the side of the road. If I saw anyone hiding in the car while the date came in to pick up Abby, I was to report back. I was young (nine years old) and did as I was told. Mom did not trust that Abby was being truthful. She believed that Abby's boyfriend was using a decoy to pick her up and that he was hiding in the car, or possibly up the street. After Abby drove away with her date, Mom called the police. The police pulled the car over, found two boys inside the car, and returned Abby home. Typical teenage defiance, sneakiness, dishonesty, and pushing adult boundaries became a nightmare. Rather than talking with Abby, Mom called the police. Lying, obfuscating, and lack of trust was a way of life for our family.

Less than two weeks later, Mom pulled Abby out of high school, told her that she would be doing home schooling by correspondence, and made her apply for a job at a hamburger drive in—which Abby did. Now Abby was trapped between work and home. There were no buses to get out of our tiny community. Abby stayed at home and worked until a month after her seventeenth birthday, when she moved out to live alone in an apartment. After living alone for six months, her older boyfriend moved in with her. The following year, they had a son.

I don't think Mom realized that having me spy and tattle on Abby did not help foster closeness and trust; it pitted us against each other. My siblings hardly knew me. Because they all left home when I was young, I did not develop close relationships with them. As adults, we divided into groups: Some of us fought with each other; others distanced ourselves. It is only in these later years of our lives that these relationships are being repaired.

After Debbie, Mary, and Abby moved out, it was just Rita, Randy, Mom, and me left at home. Then, in July 1973, Mom married a longtime friend who owned a cattle ranch five hundred miles north in a remote part of B.C. I had just finished grade seven, Rita had finished grade ten, and Randy had graduated from grade twelve. Rita and Randy remained in our family home, and I moved north with Mom to live on the cattle ranch. Even though I was pulled out of my community, away from all my friends, playmates, and siblings, I thought it would be a new and cool adventure.

In the autumn of the second year after Mom and I moved up north, she and her new husband, Richard, decided to return to Boundary Bay to check on Randy and Rita. Rita was not home when they arrived. When Rita walked in through the back door, Mom flew into a rage and began beating her. Rita fell to the floor. Richard pulled Mom off of her. Mom threatened to pull Rita out of grade twelve and send her to secretarial school. Rita refused; she was determined to finish high school. Consequently, on Thanksgiving weekend in October, 1974, Mom told Rita she was to move in with Grandma Rose. At twenty, Rita married her boyfriend of five years.

Randy remained in the house in Boundary Bay and worked as a painter, painting apartments and houses. After much soul searching, he finally secured a position as a firefighter with the local fire department. At twenty-one, he married Stella, his girlfriend and a long-time friend of Rita's. Even though all of my siblings and I experienced a lot of dysfunctional parenting and family violence, my siblings seem to have all turned out to be honest, hardworking, caring people who lovingly support their own families and communities. As for me, well, you are reading about it.

So, a long chapter in our lives ended, and a new one began. In the next chapter I will share anecdotes of my northern adventure and relate a few more defining events from my teen years, along with a summary of beliefs, thoughts, and emotions that were imprinted and imbedded into my subconscious. These formed the foundation from which I constructed and created my overarching worldview. From this outlook, I made decisions that created my personal experiences throughout my life, right up until my fifty-seventh year—when I found myself sitting at that table, writing my suicide note. I didn't know it at the time, but I was creating my every tomorrow.

Chapter 3

THE EARLY TEEN YEARS

A man should look for what is,
and not for what he thinks should be.[6]

—Albert Einstein

In early July 1973, Mom and I packed up the things we wanted to move first and headed north. Richard, my soon-to-be stepfather, my sister Rita, and her friend Stella made the trek with us. Rita and Stella were coming for Richard and Mom's wedding and to visit our new digs.

Richard was a widower of ten-plus years with a brood of six children: five boys and one girl. The youngest, Jack, is thirteen years my senior. There were roughly two years between each child. Other than Nicholas, his second youngest, who lived on the homestead, all of them had left home years earlier.

Richard's cattle ranch was in the Chilcotin district in the Central Interior of B.C., in Chezacut, 130 miles west of Williams Lake. The first fourteen miles to the ranch was paved highway;

the next eighty-six miles was gravel road; and the last thirty miles was dirt on a bed of clay. Chezacut is an unincorporated community of four ranches, on the north shore of Chilcotin Lake near the confluence of the Chilcotin and Clusko Rivers. Its name means "bird without wings" in the Chilcotin First Nation language.

In or around 1914, Richard's parents and his family had moved from Ashcroft to start a ranching operation on a property bordering Chezacut Lake. Richard's uncle owned most of the ranch land in Chezacut and had settled there in the 1800s. By 1927, Richard's parents had purchased two additional properties, one of them being a portion of the uncle's ranch. The aggregate ranch acreage was now in the order of 7,500 acres. In 1915, Richard's brother Bob was born, and two years later, Richard was born. Richard's parents operated a successful ranching operation and passed the ranch over to the two boys in 1938 with an equal split. Richard kept the uncle's homestead, associated horse-drawn carriages, and haying equipment. Later on, as Richard's family grew, he added rooms to the (uncle's) original log cabin, increasing both its size and footprint.

I found myself in a whole new environment, with *rudimentary amenities*—it was a *stark contrast* from the modern home and conveniences of our former suburban life. The nearest post office was thirty miles south, in the small community of Redstone. What follows is a description of my new environment so you can appreciate the stark contrast from childhood suburban life to this isolated and somewhat primitive existence.

The ranch ran 500 head of Hereford cattle and 130 head of horses. Richard owned a beautiful prize stallion for breeding and eighteen Hereford bulls. The lands surrounding the homestead consisted of 3,700 acres; about 1,000 of those acres were pine forest, and 2,700 acres were natural hay meadows. About seven miles from the homestead, an additional 2,700 acres of natural hay meadows bordered Chezacut Lake, Richard's parents' first purchase. Eleven miles farther was the bottom end of the range. (The entire range was twenty miles wide and thirty miles long.) The range was grazing land in the spring, summer, and early fall. In the late fall, the livestock returned to the homestead to be wintered, and calving started in late March. In May, the new calves were branded before we drove the herd to the top end of the range, where they spent the summer grazing and breeding before they returned home on their own, in about October of each year. By late October or early November, we would ride the entire range looking for stragglers that did not come home with the rest of the herd.

Mom and Richard's wedding was held in Williams Lake in early July 1973. After the reception, we drove to the ranch and unloaded our stuff. The house was a typical, one-story sprawling log home. The house was log, pure and simple, with no insulation in the walls or ceiling. The original sod roof had been covered over with a wooden frame and four-by-eight-foot sheets of aluminum. The log walls were chinked with a mixture of clay, lime, and sand, plus some cement-like compound. It was a cool house in summer; a very cold house in winter.

The house was roughly forty feet wide and 110 feet long; the floors were rough-cut logs of various sizes, nailed together. The small gaps between the floor boards and the roughness of the finish made it impossible to sweep and clean thoroughly. There were four bedrooms at the west end of the house, two to a side, with a large family room separating them. At the opposite, eastern end of the house was a living room and the master bedroom. The living room was adjacent to the dining room, which sat twelve people around a long, rectangular table. Between the living room and the large family room was a spacious kitchen, a bathroom, and a thick-walled, insulated pantry. The washing machine was in a room beside the kitchen, accessible from the family room.

All the heating and cooking was done with wood stoves. There was a large wood stove for heating in the family room, a wood stove for cooking in the kitchen, and another wood stove for heating the living room. We had a three-hundred-imperial-gallon water tank on the roof of the house above the kitchen. The tank was in an insulated, box-like structure, heated by the kitchen stove to keep it from freezing in the winter. The water tank fed potable water, via gravity, to the kitchen, bathroom, and clothes washer and was only used for washing and bathing. The tank was filled from a thirty-foot-deep well via a gas-motor-driven pump and one-and-a-half-inch-thick, heavy, somewhat flexible plastic pipe. It was a manual process to hook up and fill the tank every time it needed it. This became one of my "on-demand" tasks. Our hot water tank was heated by the kitchen stove.

Our drinking water came from a hand-operated pump at the well and sat in a galvanized, two-imperial-gallon pail on the kitchen counter. It was everyone's job to fill it as needed. A soup ladle hung on the side of the pail to fill glasses, the kettle, or pots for cooking. We had a single-cylinder diesel Lister motor driving a generator to produce 120-volt electrical power for lighting and to run an electric chest freezer and small electric tools. This was an old, old Lister motor that had two large flywheels set on protruding ends of the crankshaft on either side of the motor. It was started by attaching a hand crank to the crankshaft and turning it rapidly. The generator was noisy and only ran for a few hours each evening. It was not high-quality power—the bare incandescent light bulbs pulsed with each piston revolution. Mostly we used oil-filled lamps for light. About seventy feet from the west end of the house, near the shed that housed the generator, was the two-seater outhouse. It was a long, frosty trek to the outhouse in mid-winter.

There were two other smaller homes on the property. One was a cabin with bunk beds for housing the summer haying crew temporarily; the other was a large, one-room log cabin about thirty square feet with an internal partition separating the one bedroom from the rest of the cabin. This cabin housed the second youngest of Richard's six children, Nicholas. Nicholas was twenty-eight years old and he and his wife, Hildie, a wonderful First Nation woman, had two children, a boy (four years old) and a girl (two years old). In addition, the homestead had a large, single-car structure, without a door, that housed Richard's pickup truck. A small dilapidated shed housed a few bags of grain and other tack for the saddle horses. A large, equally dilapidated shop held various equipment: anvils, a gas-powered mobile electric arc welder, some large bottles of butane for gas welding, and other sundry ranch equipment and tools.

Just thirty feet north of the main home's kitchen door was the large gate entry into the one-and-a-half-acre pen that housed six saddle horses. This pen was large enough for self-motivated exercise and play ... horsing around, as it were. In addition to the horse pen, there were two smaller pens for grouping the animals, breeding, and training. There was no barn for any of the livestock, including the horses. The horses needed to be acclimated to the seasonal weather so they could be useful all year round, in all types of weather. We rode the horses regularly, almost daily, year-round, regardless of the weather, one hundred degrees Fahrenheit or thirty below. When it got colder than thirty below, we stayed indoors. Our lives revolved around daily feeding and watering of the horses and cows, checking on the herds by horseback, chopping or retrieving firewood, or making required trips to the outhouse. Thirty below brings a whole new meaning to "cold toilet seat."

Temperatures in Chezacut typically ranged between highs in the mid-eighties in summer to lows in the minus-twenties, with occasional drops to minus thirty (and a few spells of minus forty) in winter. For two or three days one winter, it dropped to minus sixty on our outdoor thermometer. It routinely dropped to freezing at night in late August or early September. It would warm up each day to above freezing into late December. Then winter began in earnest. Snowfall typically started around Christmas, and the snow began to melt in April each year. Cows and horses were wintered at the homestead and needed to be fed every day regardless of what Mother Nature threw at us. Of course, just like the horses, the cattle needed to be able to withstand all-weather conditions, so they too were wintered outdoors in a large field that had access to free-flowing spring water. This watering hole froze over in the winter and needed to be chopped free of ice every day in the winter.

All year long I was assigned the task of chopping blocks of wood with a double-bitted axe to feed the kitchen stove. This stove alone consumed about sixty cords of wood per year and weekly (many times bi-weekly), I was out splitting the wood. The stoves at either end of the house accepted logs that were cut eighteen inches or shorter, lengthwise. As I mentioned, these two stoves were the only heat source for the house, and in the fall, winter, and spring, they needed to be fed throughout the night to keep the bedrooms habitable. My bedroom was in the southwest corner of the house and had a single-pane window in the southern wall. Initially, I had my bed beside the outside wall until one morning in the dead of winter, I woke up with my sheets frozen to the wall. I moved my bed.

The homestead was in a remote area, comprising four ranches and their families and four distantly scattered homes of First Nation families (i.e., indigenous peoples). These First Nation folks lived off-reserve; the nearest reserve was about thirty miles away. The closest First Nation family to us lived just outside the western boundaries of our ranch; the rest were four or more miles away. The ranchers were older folks with full-grown children who had young children of their own. Richard's older brother, Bob, lived about seven miles from our homestead with his second family—he and his wife had six kids ranging in age from five to twenty-one. Bob's first wife had left him, taking their youngest of five children, Vinnie, about four years old, with her. Each of the First Nation families had lots of children with kids under twenty.

In all of the Chezacut population, there was no one my age. Mom was the principal and teacher at the local school and taught grades one to seven. There were two kids in grade seven that were close to my age, but I did not hang out with anyone. Other than my youngest stepbrother, Jack, thirteen years my senior, I had no close relationships. Jack was married to a First Nations woman, Opal. They had a newborn baby girl; they called her Christina. Although Jack had left the ranch a few years to earlier to go logging, he agreed to come back and help at the ranch for a year and a bit. He and his family arrived in early September 1973 and left again in November 1974. I learned a lot from him in that year, and we became very close. He was like the protective older brother I never had. He taught me how to ride, hunt, gut a moose, drive a car, drive a tractor, sleep in the bush without a tent, and do leather work, to name a few handy skills to have when living in a remote place.

When Jack, Opal, and Christina moved away so he could resume his logging career, I became a loner; self-reliant and self-sufficient. It was a different life to the one I had led in Boundary Bay, when up to grade seven, I'd had many close friends, participated in school activities and community activities, and played team sports.

In this new environment, my experiences further shaped and strengthened my foundation and my views of the world.

Soon after we arrived, Mom made a list of home improvements she wanted to make to increase the house's habitability. Within a week, she and Richard made the trek to Williams Lake to pick up the materials. Two primary changes included hanging wallpaper in the kitchen and dining room, and installing four-by-eight-foot sheets of hardboard to cover all the flooring in the house. The hardboard was clear-coated three times with an oil-based, clear Varathane. The brown hardboard matched the color of the aged logs well—and we could now sweep and wash the floors. It was a good choice.

By the third week of July, Mom, Richard, Rita, and Stella had headed back to Boundary Bay to gather another load of our belongings. Rita and Stella would not be coming back. I was left behind with the understanding that Mom and Richard would be back in a week to ten days. As I mentioned earlier, Nicholas lived about a hundred feet away in his own small home, and he promised to take care of me and ensure I came to no harm. I prepared and cooked my own meals, cleaned up the dishes and the house, visited Nicholas and his family, played outside, explored the property on foot, or stayed at home and read. There was a black-and-white TV with one channel that worked … some of the time. The sound was consistently clear and audible, but the picture came through only periodically. Since the TV's operation relied on electricity, it was daylight until late in the day, and the generator was not run often, TV watching was not really "a thing." I was thirteen, and this was a great opportunity to be independent and self-sufficient.

We had no telephone. The only way for us to receive one-way communications was through the Williams Lake Radio station. Every day at thirteen hundred hours, messages were broadcast to listeners from family, friends, and visitors regarding important things. For example, when someone was going to be arriving in Chezacut, they would phone the radio station and broadcast a message informing the recipients that they could be expected to arrive on a particular day at a particular time.

By the end of the second week, Mom and Richard had not returned. I listened to the radio every day, but there was no message. I started to worry. Nicholas tried to reassure me. "Everything's fine," he said. "Probably, they're just delayed a day or two. They'll show up any day now."

The days and weeks clicked by—still no message. I was beyond worried. *What if they'd died in a car crash and never come back?* I wondered. I had never been left alone for a day, let alone weeks on end. I did not drive, had no car, and was miles from civilization, and there was no way to communicate with anyone outside of a face-to-face meeting. Sure, Nicholas and his family were next door, but their way of life was entirely foreign to me. I was anxious and somewhat fearful; I had no confidant to console me or make me feel safe.

Then the government-issued "dole" arrived. All the local, non-employed First Nations families received it—the more kids a family had, the higher their income. A day later, the bootleggers arrived. Money and booze exchanged hands, and Nicholas and Hildie, their kids, and I all piled into his pickup truck and headed over to her family's cabin by the river. Anyone over the age of fifteen, Hildie's brothers and sisters included, enjoyed copious quantities of cheap Kelowna red wine. Everyone (except me) drank until they passed out, then they woke up and drank some more. After two days, Nicholas packed us up to go home. Some of the family followed, red wine in tow. We headed back to the homestead; they carried on at Nicholas' house. I had never experienced being around anyone drunk in my entire life. I had seen some inebriated partygoers at my mother's wedding reception, but that was brief. Having an immersive, extended experience around drunks (and relying on them for transport) was new and scary for me. I escaped to my house and locked myself in.

Over the following week, I ventured out cautiously during the day, going to the outhouse only as required and retrieving fresh water from the well whenever I needed to refill the bucket. The pantry was well-stocked with dry goods, canned food, and smoked meat, so I could feed myself without issue. Now and then I checked in at Nicholas' place to see if the partying had ended. Their "drunk" lasted about a week until the wine ran out. Mom and Richard still had not returned. In the middle of the night, I routinely heard coyotes howling. At first this was a little scary, but I soon got used to it. It was so strange to not have electricity. In the night, I either had to light a kerosene lamp or use a flashlight to get a drink of water. Outhouse trips were another story. I imagined all kinds of menacing things coming to attack me: coyotes, bears, or other creatures. I was frantic with worry, alone, and frightened. My novels kept my mind active, and I would read whatever I could find lying around the house; usually a cowboy adventure of some kind or other. I tried to make the best of it.

After about a five-week absence, Mom and Richard finally showed up, unannounced, with no excuses and no explanations ... other than "It took longer to sort everything out." Richard's retort to my predicament was, "Aw, it's good for him. It builds character." I know (now) he meant well. They had a pickup truck full of provisions and my mother's belongings. At that moment, I was so glad to see them that all my feelings of abandonment and fear fell away. But I can see now that all those weeks of isolation, loneliness, and solitude; not knowing what would happen; whether they were alive or dead; or if my mom would ever return for me were immensely impactful. *If they had been hospitalized or had died in a car crash, how would I have known? Who would tell me? How would I get home? Who would look after me?* All these questions remained unspoken and unresolved. I had been abandoned, and it threatened my inner security and safety so thoroughly that again, I planted another fearful, potent seed in my subconscious mind.

Mom was principal and teacher at the remote, one-room elementary school. About four miles from the ranch, the school was a pre-built building that had been trucked into Chezacut and assembled on a concrete foundation. It had one bathroom with a toilet, hand sink, and large utility sink; there was a storage room for supplies; and a large front door with a foyer that had wall hooks for hanging coats. There was an outbuilding alongside it that housed a large, diesel-generating unit that provided electricity. There was a teacher's one-bedroom, one-bathroom single-wide mobile home about twenty feet from main building, which Mom used for storing personal teaching supplies. Well water was supplied automatically by an electrically operated pump. Both the school and the trailer had electric hot water tanks, and both buildings were heated by electric baseboard heaters.

I was starting grade eight, the first year of high school. The nearest high school was in Williams Lake, but instead of sending me to board there (or elsewhere), Mom decided I would do home correspondence. For most of that year I did my lessons by going to and from school with her each day and working on my correspondence courses alone in the mobile home. Did I mention it too had an indoor toilet, electricity, and running water? That was a real treat!

Mom secured the position of school janitor for me as an after-school job. She and I typically ate lunch together in the trailer, and after Mom finished teaching each day, while I cleaned the school, she marked papers and prepared lessons for the next day. I made about four hundred dollars a month. I was frugal with my money, and it all went into the bank. Over time, I saved up enough to buy a couple of new rifles and a saddle. The rest I kept in an interest-bearing savings account.

Before the school year ended, I became restless with the daily trek and struck an agreement with Mom to do my lessons at home, as well as do the house cleaning as a trade-off for not coming to the school to do the janitorial work. It was more work to clean the house, but less time was wasted traveling. This benefited Mom too, as she had less work to do at home. She still paid me the monthly janitorial income.

We set up a small desk in my bedroom, and I fell into a routine—starting school in October each year, finishing by the end of March, and working on lessons for four hours each weekday. Virtually every afternoon I was on my horse—his name was Donald—riding, hunting, fishing, or just exploring. Unless it was colder than twenty below Fahrenheit, I was out.

In the winter my mode of transportation varied—either snowmobile or my trusty steed, Donald. Horseback was by far my preferred mode of transportation. I loved the peacefulness, the creak of the saddle, Donald's snorts, the solitude of riding. I told no one where I was going or when I would be home. In retrospect, it seems odd. No one ever inquired. Most of the time, I didn't even know where I was going. I would just get on Donald, pick a direction, and ride for hours. I'd make my way down to the Chezacut River and ice fish in the winter, or open water fly or spin cast in the warmer months. Rainbow trout, Dolly Varden, or whitefish were the catch all year round; returning-to-spawn Chinook salmon were the main event in the fall.

In the fall and spring, waterfowl were available wherever there was a lake. We had two small lakes out back on the homestead and in the spring, we dammed up a creek that ran through the hayfield to flood it. These water bodies were rife with waterfowl. (In the 1990s, Richard sold the ranch to Ducks Unlimited and it is now a permanently flooded, three-thousand-acre waterfowl extravaganza.)

My days were my own. I did well in my school lessons; I got straight A's across the board. The correspondence lessons seemed so easy, I thought I must be receiving a substandard education. I wondered, had I attended a real school, would I have failed miserably? Or, at a minimum, would I have fallen behind my cohorts?

In the spring of that first year in Chezacut, I had a confrontation with a First Nation boy named Freddy. He was thin, not very muscular, and an inch or two shorter than me. I don't remember what it was about, but I remember pinning him up against a wall at the school and telling him, "If you ever do that again, I will beat the crap out of you." I was not a violent person, but I could threaten with the best of them. Up to that point in my life, other than having been beaten up by my older brother occasionally, I had been in exactly three fights with schoolmates. In grade three, a good friend, Harold, who had taken boxing lessons, punched me in the mouth during recess. He was in grade four and bigger than me. That one punch was the end of the fight. The second time, in grade six, another good friend and I rolled around on the floor at school, working to overpower each other … in the end, it was a draw. The third time was in the gym, and my assailant punched me in the privates, bringing a short confrontation to a quick and painful end for me.

Back to Freddy. The incident was short and was never broached between us again. However, during a week-long drunk at Nicholas' place the following summer, I ventured over one morning to see what was going on. Freddy's dad, Andy, was sitting on the sofa, as drunk as everyone else. Andy was in his early forties, with a stocky build. About four inches taller than me, he was normally shy, reserved, and politely spoken. It was mid-morning, and everyone was still able to stand and talk somewhat coherently. I greeted everyone; they were all sitting on the sofa. As I stood, talking with Nicholas and Hildie, I noticed Andy staring at me with disdain. He stood up and came toward me.

About five feet from me, he barked, "You threatened Freddy!" Then he drew a six-inch, fixed-blade hunting knife from its scabbard and lunged at me. I jumped backward quickly, turned, and ran around to the other side of the kitchen table. Andy was hot in pursuit. As Andy chased me around that table, brandishing his knife wildly, Nicholas remained sitting on the sofa, laughing. I was terrified. Andy screamed, repeatedly trying to knife me. On the fourth time around the table, I dashed for the door. Thankfully, it was slightly ajar. I thrust it open, and leaping down the two steps leading up into the house, I ran into the expanse of the yard. Andy gave up chasing me. I ran home. I did not speak a word of this to anyone, ever. I held it inside. After that incident, I was always extremely cautious and afraid whenever I encountered Andy. I always kept my distance. Fear had not only struck at my heart; it coursed violently through my veins.

Thus, another seed was planted—a seed that grew into a strong need for control. I needed to be sure that there would never be any surprises, I needed to know in intimate detail what lay ahead. I was hypervigilant. Alert to the possibility of danger around every corner, I trusted no one and no thing ... I became self-sufficient and self-reliant, a survivor at all costs. That incident with Andy was the final affront: No one and nothing could reach me.

Chapter 4

THE LATE TEEN YEARS

Health, wealth, beauty, and genius are not created; they are only manifested by the arrangement of your mind— that is, by your concept of yourself, and your concept of yourself is all that you accept and consent to as true.[7]

—Neville Goddard

Living in Chezacut with Mom and Richard required serious stocking of provisions. Buying provisions meant a 130-mile trek to Williams Lake, so typically, canned and dried goods were stocked to last three months at a time. Fresh meat was wild game or fish. Once a year, we slaughtered a cow. When stocks ran low, Mom and Richard would head into Williams Lake, and I always wanted to go. It was a chance "to get into Dodge," to be part of civilization, to shop for clothes and food, and to eat in a restaurant. Each trip required at least one night's stay at the Lakeview Hotel, sometimes two nights depending on what we needed to get or with whom we needed to visit.

The three-story Lakeview Hotel had twenty rooms, a Chinese food restaurant, and a large pub. The hotel lobby (which featured an old, brown two-seater sofa) separated the restaurant and the pub. The pub was the local watering hole and had lots of regulars, including Richard when he was in town. A functioning alcoholic, Richard could refrain from drinking. However, these trips were opportunities to meet up with his friends and other ranchers also in town gathering supplies. Richard was well known in the region; in his youth, he had been a Williams Lake Rodeo Saddle Bronc Champion. Consequently, after they had gathered provisions, he and Mom left me on the hotel lobby sofa and went to the pub for a visit with friends—and a "one-for-the-road" event. I had nowhere to go and knew no one. So, for three to five hours, I sat. Every hour or so, a server would bring me a glass of coke. As it grew both later and darker (especially in the wintertime), Mom and Richard would finally emerge. Richard was always piss drunk, and while Mom seemed sober, I'm sure she was slightly inebriated. She always tried to get the truck keys from Richard, but he became belligerent. He was of the mind that if you are *too drunk to walk, you can always drive.*

The three of us would pile into the single cab of the pickup, Mom in the middle, and away we would go. By the time we got home, three hours later, Richard would be reasonably sober. To this day, I am amazed we never got pulled over, got into an accident, or died in a horrific crash.

After two years of being around this never-ending alcoholic behavior, I detested anyone who drank alcohol. By the age of fifteen, I loathed drinkers—more specifically, drunks. Another seed sown. I also developed a driving, compelling need to always be in control of my circumstances and environment, regardless of the situation.

After finishing grade nine, I wanted nothing more than to get out of Chezacut. I wanted to go back to Boundary Bay, back to my community, my friends, my sports, and a proper school with actual teachers. That summer, I took an entrance exam for a prestigious boys-only boarding school on Vancouver Island. I passed the exam, and Mom took me to an interview. It was a five-hundred-mile road trip back to Boundary Bay, then a ninety-five-minute ferry ride to Vancouver Island, then forty miles to the school. What an adventure we had!

The headmaster showed me around the school and gave me a thorough overview of the rules, expectations, and daily activities. He showed me the dorm rooms, the communal areas, the eating hall, and the group bathrooms and showers. The interview went well. I was accepted into the school.

While the school's focus was on academics, everyone had to participate in sports, be it basketball, rugby, soccer, or track and field. Going to the school meant I would have to wear shorts, share a shower with others, and sleep in a room with three other boys. I remained self-consciousness about my previous chubbiness and still did not want—ever—to be seen in public in shorts. I imagined hearing a chanting chorus by my new schoolmates of the "Fatty, fatty two-by-four" song. I wouldn't have been able to bear it. Going there also meant that I would be nowhere near Boundary Bay and that I would only see my family at Christmas, Easter, Thanksgiving, and summer vacations. I was not up for this arrangement and decided, as much as I despised the thought, to spend another year in Chezacut, completing grade ten by correspondence. I see now that the seed of fear linked to abandonment, along with my shame about my body, drove this decision. Mom wouldn't let me, at age fifteen, live on my own in the house in Boundary Bay, and living with my grandmother was apparently not an option. So, I faced another winter of twenty-to-forty-below weather, no friends, and lobby sofas.

I stuck it out—one more school year in Chezacut. That winter, I visited Bob's family more often than I had in the past, at least four or five times by horseback or tractor, to play cards in the basement with his children. His oldest son, Wade, twenty-one, had stocks of booze ... Canadian Club rye whiskey (the drink of choice for cowboys in the area), beer, vodka, rum. One time, I got very drunk on rye, and though I made it home, I was sick and felt terrible. From then on, I stuck to having a beer now and then. I wasn't a big drinker and despised alcoholics when they brought out the booze, not because they were alcoholics but because they just couldn't stop until the bottle ... or bottles ... were empty.

I spent that winter like I'd spent the last one, from October to March, doing four hours a day of school work and riding, hunting, and fishing the rest of the time.

By March, I was done with the isolation. I was bitter, belligerent, and unruly; anger seeped out of every pore. One of Richard's older sons, Matthew, had purchased a ranch and a guiding/hunting outfit in Progress, B.C., with territory in the Murray River area of the Rocky Mountains. He bought six unbroken horses from Richard and asked me if I would come with him to help him break the horses, both for riding and as pack horses. I jumped at the chance.

In early April, we loaded up the horses and headed to his new place. We drove a relatively small 1960's dual-wheel truck with a box just big enough for the six horses, comfortably spaced but not a lot of room between the animals. The horses could see out without putting their heads outside of the box, and the box provided fresh airflow so they would not overheat on a hot day. The weather was above freezing and comfortable, so they would be okay on the trip.

We left Chezacut mid-afternoon on a warm spring day. The snow was starting to melt, and the roads were getting muddy. It was going to be a ten- to eleven-hour trip, and Matthew had planned to drive all night to make it home by the following day. By 1:00 a.m., we were climbing a steep grade to a summit known as Pine Pass; we were about 70 percent through our journey. The weather had turned, with temperatures dropping to thirty below Fahrenheit. We had to go slowly so as not to freeze the horses. Fortunately, they were huddled together in the small box; that helped keep them warm.

Suddenly, the motor started to overheat. We were in the middle of nowhere in the middle of the night. We hadn't seen another car or truck in two or three hours. Matthew slowed right down, saying that there was a homestead by the highway within the next mile or two. We made it. We pulled into the large gravel parking spot, turned off the motor, and stared at the completely dark home. No cars or trucks in sight. No choice.

Crossing our fingers and holding our breath, we headed to the front door and knocked loudly. Within a few minutes, a man opened the door. We apologized for disturbing him at such a late hour and explained our situation. He topped us up with enough water to keep the motor running at the proper temperature and prepared some fresh coffee for Matthew and me. Matthew tried to pay him for his generosity, but he would not accept it. We thanked him profusely and headed out. We made it to Matthew's ranch at four in the morning. His wife greeted us; their three kids were still sleeping. We unloaded the horses and went to bed.

That spring and summer, I helped break Matthew's horses and acted as a ranch hand. We also cut numerous trails in the Murray River hunting territory for the fall hunting guides. It was a wild region; the grizzly bears there had never seen a human being. The bush was thick; you couldn't see more than six to ten feet in front of you. Consequently, my 30-06 rifle was my constant companion. "Load it; carry it with you everywhere," Matthew told me. "Even sleep with it on the trail." Thankfully, I never had to use it. In truth, at that close a range, a semi-automatic twelve-gauge shotgun would have been a better choice, but we only had our rifles.

By the end of the summer, I had earned and saved enough money to buy a new car. I had turned sixteen that spring and got my learner's license. I headed back to Richard's ranch to go back to school. I made an agreement with Mom that I would complete one more year of correspondence and stay at Chezacut. That September, I took a few driving lessons and passed my driver's test. I ordered a brand-new, 1976 four-wheel drive, three-quarter-ton GMC pickup from the factory. It had an expected delivery date of early- to mid-December.

As luck would have it, that fall I could not do math eleven without instruction, and there was no one locally who could instruct me. This idea of me not finishing grade twelve was a non-starter for Mom, so she agreed I could live on my own in the house in Boundary Bay and start high school in Tsawwassen in January. My four-by-four black pickup truck was delivered to me one mid-day in mid-December. I loaded all my possessions into the eight-foot box, threw a large canvas tarp over it, and late that same afternoon, I headed home to Boundary Bay. I stayed in a motel in Cache Creek overnight and got up at five in the morning to finish the journey.

Once I had unloaded my truck, I set myself up in my old bedroom. I had a two-story, five-bedroom, one-bathroom home to myself. My brother and his wife, Stella, were still renting the small, attached but separate home from Mom. This arrangement was going to suit me just fine.

Mom and Richard came down for Christmas, and I was registered to start high school in January 1977. I was given an allowance of three hundred dollars a month and I agreed to be responsible; not have parties, take care of the house, keep out of trouble, attend school, and do my lessons. Finally, I was home!

On the first day of school, I wore my cowboy best. Jeans, large shiny cowboy buckle on my belt, cowboy boots, cowboy shirt with snaps, and a cowboy hat. I drove the three miles to school, my excitement mixed with a generous dose of trepidation. While I still knew a number of people from elementary school, this high school was an amalgamation of all the elementary schools in the region, so the total grade eleven class size would top four hundred students—many of whom I did not know. I arrived in my pickup and found a spot in the parking lot among the variety of cars. Late 1960's and early 1970's traditional family cars were sprinkled between a smattering of muscle cars: Dodge Challengers, Ford Mustangs, Chevy Chevelles, Plymouth Road Runners, Chevy Camaros, and Plymouth Barracudas. The only other pickup trucks in sight were driven by gardening crews or city workers. I went to the school office, was oriented to the rules and layout of the school, and given a quick tour. I buddied up with a friend, Steven, whom I had known since childhood. Steven showed me around and pointed me to my classes. Our lockers were in relative proximity. I left my hat in my locker and attended my classes.

Now and then I had a class where I actually knew someone, but for the most part, everyone was new to me. Everyone was nice, but I was a fish out of water. I had been acclimated to the north and cowboy mannerisms. It was the first time I had ever attended a high school. Shy and reserved, I made few friends that semester.

An outcast and not accepted by the "cool kids" or the jocks, I didn't play sports. My mental image of being fat and looking chubby in shorts (although I wasn't fat at all) continued. Everyone was pleasant, and it helped that I already knew a few friends from elementary school. But I had changed from the once gregarious, fun-loving joker who loved attention to a shy, reserved cowboy who lacked social skills. The popular set saw me as an oddball with my cowboy hat and boots and my four-by-four pickup. The students that did accept me were my few friends from the past and those that might be called "misfits." They liked to party with alcohol and recreational drugs. I still had a beer now and then, but this group introduced me to drugs. I started smoking cigarettes at the same time too—and became a chain-smoker.

The drug use started with an offer to smoke a joint. When I lived up north, I never dreamed of trying drugs. It was not looked upon favorably, and well, it was just not an option. Over a one-year period in grade eleven and twelve, the array of drugs I tried increased. If I could smoke it, snort it, or swallow it, it was fair game—although I never tried anything that required needles. I liked recreational drugs ... I felt in control, and ... no hangover. I figured, hey, high on grass, I am more likely to get pulled over for driving too slowly than for speeding or driving erratically. So, since I lived alone, I invited small groups of friends over to get high or have a few beers.

Thinking back, I was pretty responsible for a teenager who lived alone. I had strict house rules—I was my own parent, and my rules were simple: Shoes off at the door. Take empty bottles with you when you go. Empty your ashtrays. Rinse your dirty glasses or dishes and put them in the dishwasher. All garbage in the proper trash bin. No unruly behavior, yelling, or fighting. I never had more than four friends over at a time. Without exception, everyone respected the rules—they knew that if they didn't, they wouldn't be invited back. I was not their parent and I refused to clean up after them.

Meanwhile, my marijuana use increased. By the time I graduated from grade twelve, I was high most days. I woke up, smoked a joint, then got out of bed. By the time I turned nineteen, the dope and chain-smoking two packs of cigarettes a day had started to take their toll on my lungs. I remember waking up coughing up black tar. One day I coughed up tar and said to myself, "This is crazy—I'm killing myself!" I had to give up the dope or the cigarettes. I threw the pack of eighteen cigarettes into the fireplace and quit. It was hard to resist having a smoke for a few months, especially when I had a coffee or sat with a friend over a beer, but I had made up my mind.

Despite hanging out sometimes with my small group of drug-smoking buddies, after I moved back to Boundary Bay, I was alone most of the time. I was not only alone; I was lonely. Up north I was always out on my own but came home to family—we'd play pool, watch the snowy TV together, or play cards. I could go into my bedroom and read, knowing there were other people around. If I had an issue, there was always someone to talk to.

I had a lot of freedom living alone. My brother and I were not close. I certainly wouldn't confide anything personal to him. He liked to leave me alone, and I was good with that. I had some dinners with them and visited with his wife, Stella, now and then. But it was not a loving, close, protective, older-brother relationship. I had no trusted family to talk to and was never comforted by the knowledge that there was someone there in the next room. I lacked confidence. I was shy and awkward around girls I liked and wanted to date.

In March 1977, I finally worked up the courage to ask a girl out on a date. Karen was a year younger than me, and we dated for about five months. She was about my height, with shoulder-length dark hair, and she was well endowed (if you get my drift), small-waisted, and had nice hips. She was, in my eyes, gorgeous. She liked to laugh, watch TV, was playful, and was sexually adventurous, once we actually started that activity. That took a while. We were always together. My loneliness disappeared. Her parents were nice people in their forties. They lived a half-mile from my house. Karen had a younger brother, Roger, who was fun, confident, and gregarious. Their father was a commercial airline pilot. The family were generous and welcomed me. I felt like I belonged—and I was in love.

In August of that year, however, suddenly, Karen's parents vehemently discouraged our relationship. Karen wanted to have a baby; I just wanted to continue having sex. I believed that from Karen's point of view, I needed to agree to the baby or my sex life was over. We did not practise the proper protective protocols—Karen's mother found out—and that was the end of our relationship. She was forbidden to see me. It was the best for both of us, really. We were just teenagers, clueless about the responsibilities of having a child and the kind of life we would have created for ourselves. I was heartbroken. As before, I had no one to confide in or talk to, no one to console me. My loneliness came back with a vengeance.

In September, I entered grade twelve. Back in high school, no distractions, no girlfriend, no real social life … I was back into my routine. My loneliness was palpable. I can see now that my increased drug use was to combat loneliness. It was effective but not life-giving or life-affirming. My motivation to do anything of value in life waned. I hated school. I did not want to go to university.

In late June, right after graduation, I got a well-paying labor job on the green line with a fly-in northern B.C. sawmill. The mill produced railway ties with a secondary product of two-by-fours. Workers spent ten days in camp, working ten-hour days, then flew out of the camp for four days of rest and relaxation. With nowhere to spend money and all food and board paid for, I saved a goodly sum. And ten hours a day juggling lumber by hand built up great muscle strength; I felt fit and strong. When I was on leave and back in Boundary Bay, I ran into a friend from high school, who commented on how huge my arms were—and it was then I realized that really, my arms and upper body looked like a body builder's. But three months of standing for long periods sorting lumber wore me out; my lower back started to suffer. The money was good, but I had had enough. I quit.

I returned home to Boundary Bay and looked for another job. I worked in a local family-owned pizza parlor on the afternoon-to-closing shift as a cook, then as an afternoon janitor at the Workers Compensation Board, then sold Filter Queen vacuum cleaners door to door for commission. I completed the exam to become an air traffic controller but was not called for an interview (that might have had something to do with the joint I smoked in the parking lot before taking the exam).

When I turned eighteen, I took the entrance exam for the Vancouver Police Force. I was called for an interview and was told that the only recruit ever hired at eighteen was the police chief's son. They told me to try again in a few years. In truth, my only motivation at the time was to drive excessively fast, without getting pulled over and ticketed ... not really the substance of what makes a stellar police officer. I did not reapply.

Mom wanted me to do "something." She suggested I become a teacher, get a trade, even go to hairdressing school to become a hair stylist. I grimaced at the suggestions. Finally, when I turned nineteen, I decided to get my Class 1 driver's license, with the aspiration of driving an eighteen-wheeler rig long distance. I got my license and finally, after months of searching, got a local Vancouver job delivering concrete.

I delivered concrete for several months, hanging out with a few new friends and searching for a girl I could date. After one or two dating experiences (fun for a month or two), I met Sylvia, and we began to date. She liked to drink with friends in a bar after she got off work. Like I had done earlier, she smoked cigarettes, about a pack a day. I didn't judge her for it. Her alcohol consumption was consistent with the folks she hung out with in the bar. It's funny when I think about now, but I never recognized that the reason she went to a bar daily to drink was because she (might have) had a drinking problem.

Sylvia worked for her mom, who owned a popular ethnic restaurant in the Vancouver suburb of Richmond, not far from Boundary Bay. We dated for seven months. But I wanted to be free, spread my wings, and go to Europe on a backpacking trip. I broke up with her.

Early in my trip, I met an Australian guy in Calais, France, who was a year or two my senior. We ended up traveling together, visiting virtually every western European country, including Ireland. After he left to go back home to Sydney, I traveled to Britain and Scotland on my own. I was away for three months, and every two weeks, I wrote a letter to Sylvia. I turned twenty on a beach on Ios, Greece. It was a great experience.

But I was lonely and pined for Sylvia. Three months after I returned from Europe, in September 1980, Sylvia and I were married.

In the next chapter I share a few stories about how I navigated adulthood—always reaping, reinforcing, and replanting ingrained and embedded beliefs, thoughts, and emotions in my daily life. I was a sailboat with a full sail but no rudder. I was blown this way and that in winds of fortune and misfortune, and always, always I viewed life through the lens that I had ground: a lens of mistrust, denial, blame, and fear. I had a fear of abandonment, fear of being alone, fear of not being smart enough, fear of not being attractive, fear of not being good enough, fear of failure, fear of being judged or rejected, fear of chemicals, fear of disease, and fear of death.

I was afraid of life.

Chapter 5

ADULTHOOD

Wherever you go, there you are.[8]
—Jon Kabat-Zinn

Because a lifetime of accumulated fears ruled my every move, it makes sense to me now, looking back, that I walked right into a world of pain in my first marriage. I see now that much of what I did and most of the choices I made during this next period of my life were a result of the fear gremlins that were whispering constant doom and gloom messages in my ear. I was motivated by shame, guilt, anxiety, fear of failure—and fear of everything. I was unknowingly using my creative tools to create my every tomorrow. Below are a few more pages of detail to show how I kept digging a deeper and deeper hole for myself—a hole of depression and anguish that eventually, I fell right into and that led me to that kitchen table, pen in hand. Happily, I came to a fork in my road that led me to freedom....

Sylvia and I were young, immature emotionally and psychologically. We were not really suited to one another—that became apparent almost from the beginning. She came from a family of strong Ukrainian Catholics; I was agnostic. I was open to anything logical that made sense. I was searching for the meaning of life and with Sylvia, I could take on some form of belief. I asked to be baptized into the Ukrainian Catholic church.

I had no religious training, so I tried reading the Bible but could not understand the parables. My worldview was simplistic: I believed in heaven and hell, that marriage was a lifetime commitment, that divorce was a sin, and that committing sin would result in me going to hell at death. It was in this context that Sylvia and I got married. When we returned from our two-week honeymoon, I looked for a job.

We lived at my family's home in Boundary Bay. I drove far and wide looking for a truck-driving job, but couldn't find one. At Sylvia's prompting of "Just do something, Neil," I decided to go to university and get an engineering degree. It was one year of science and four years of engineering. I secured student loans. I applied for a January 1981 start at a college to refresh my math and English and to take the remaining subjects to fulfill the first year of science. One pre-engineering requisite course was first-year chemistry, which included learning in the classroom and through controlled experiments in the laboratory.

I liked my lab partner a lot. A wonderful young woman, Janice was kind, funny, considerate—and clumsy. One day, we were conducting an experiment that involved the highest concentration of a dangerous chemical, an inorganic base that could cause serious harm to bare skin. Janice dropped the beaker. It broke. Liquid splashed on our bare skin.

Our professor rushed over. "Wash thoroughly for five to ten minutes under cold water—now," he said.

While I washed, I kept my cool, but internally, I was freaking out. The event reinforced that seed that had been planted in my subconscious in early childhood—and in that moment, my obsessive-compulsive disorder (OCD) was born. Excessive hand-washing was the first on my list of OCD behaviors.

I completed first-year science with flying colors and secured a spot in Engineering at the University of British Columbia (UBC). Over the next four years, I drove forty minutes from Boundary Bay to UBC every morning and back again every afternoon after class. In the evenings I studied late … and then did it all over again the next day. Soon, our marriage was on rocky ground. Sylvia and I were both unhappy. She had quit her waitressing job at her mother's restaurant and could not seem to hold a job anywhere else, always complaining that she was treated badly or harassed at work. To fix things between us, we decided to start a family. I had one condition: she needed to stop drinking and stop smoking. She agreed.

She cut down on her alcohol consumption during pregnancy but never stopped smoking. Prior to the birth of our first child, I applied for life insurance. During the required medical, my doctor discovered I had a form of heart disease: a bicuspid aortic valve, with two leaflets, instead of three. My life insurance ended up being very expensive!

Sylvia and I had two beautiful children: Carmen in 1985, and James in 1987. Even though they both had the same family of origin and family environment, they were like chalk and cheese, expressing radical differences in thought and behavior. I see now that they interpreted the childhood events, discussions, and conversations they were exposed to differently. Even though they were subject to the same conditions, James and Carmen have chosen different paths in life. More about the kids later on in this timeline.

Back to me. In my third year of engineering, the curriculum required a course in microbiology; with classroom learning, homework, and laboratory work. All the students wore white lab coats and participated in laboratory experiments, studying cells, bacteria, and viruses. We grew a lot of cultures, learned how they reproduced, propagated, and spread, and studied the effects of bacteria and viruses on cells. We swabbed our mouths with medical Q-tips and grew the resulting bacteria in petri dishes—the amount of flora and fauna in one's mouth is astounding! Already virus-phobic, by the time that class was over, I had added bacteria to my ever-increasing list of fears. Another phobia and OCD seed was planted, germinated, grown, and harvested.

In 1986, I graduated with a degree in bio-resource engineering, and Sylvia and I moved our family to Toronto for my first professional job. Sadly, our marriage continued to degrade; having children had not restored our happiness. I wanted out. But I had made a commitment for life, divorce was a sin, and I knew I would pay for it when I died—so, I stayed.

In 1989, I secured a position back in Vancouver. We moved in with Sylvia's mother; her father had passed away a year earlier. After a year, I changed jobs again, this time joining a great company I could only have dreamed of working for. They paid well, had a gold-plated benefits package (including eight weeks' vacation to start and a rarely offered, defined pension plan). I was a proud employee. The internal job opportunities for personal growth seemed limitless, and over time, I moved from a technical engineering role to a project management role. This became my "bread and butter" profession. Frankly, I am very good at it. My boss put me on projects that had gone off the rails to get them back on track, on unusual or new technological projects, and on extremely complex and technically challenging projects. All my projects came in on time and on—or under—budget. Project management truly became my forte.

In the fall of 1990, I experienced chest pains and went to the doctor. They determined that the pain was nothing of concern, likely muscles in the chest wall. They did discover, however, that my heart was enlarged by 23 percent over normal and that I needed open-heart surgery to replace what was left of my aortic valve. They felt it was likely that a bout of bacterial endocarditis had fully consumed the two leaflets of the valve. I had no (or very little) valve left. They explained to me that if the heart enlarges beyond 25 percent of normal, it will never return to its normal size. It was critical, the doctors said, that I have surgery. But a hospital strike that had lasted months had canceled all surgeries in my region, and there was no end in sight for the strike. After three months of waiting and still no end to the strike, Sylvia was at the end of her rope. On the Thursday before the Easter long weekend, she called the Provincial Health Minister and did what she did best: She yelled and screamed, told him we had two young children, and said that she would go the newspapers if I did not get in for surgery.

The following day, we received a call from the hospital: My surgery was scheduled for the following Tuesday at 7:00 a.m. I was terrified, but I wanted to live. I had no options. I promised myself, "If I live through this, I'll be a better person. I'll give our marriage one year to improve. If there is no improvement, I'll get a divorce."

The surgery was successful. I was fitted with a mechanical aortic valve the surgeon said should outlast the rest of me. I returned home and each week, I attended a trial run of a new cardiac recovery exercise program. Three times a week, I had supervised nutritional and physical education with exercise training overseen by a doctor and three nurses. I learned how to exercise properly and monitor my body's responses. Running was my exercise of choice. I found it meditative. Over eighteen weeks, I ran three times a week and shed thirty-five pounds. I was fit, strong, and had never felt better in my life.

My marriage to Sylvia, however, declined. Co-dependent and absorbed in our dysfunctional relationship, I knew we were harming our children psychologically. Sylvia wasn't willing to change. She had no intention of ever holding a job or earning money. Without discussion and without an agreement between us, she felt it was her right to stay home, shop, look after the kids, smoke and drink, and buy whatever she wanted—regardless of our ever-increasing credit card and personal line of credit debt. My job was to earn the money, clean the dishes, and clean the house.

I have always been private about my personal life and was reluctant to share with (admit to, really) anyone the situation in which I found myself. But one day, over lunch with a colleague in the company cafeteria, I shared some of my home situation. "What are you teaching your children about relationships?" my co-worker asked. I felt like I'd been struck upside the head by a two-by-four! In that moment, I decided I needed to get out. The only thing left to sort out was *how*.

I did it as best I could and anticipated an amicable split. I was so wrong. Two months after I told Sylvia we should part ways, I moved out. She denied me access to James and Carmen and refused to let me have any belongings I had not already moved out of the house. She wanted to see me living under a downtown bridge, preferably with pigeons defecating on me. We went to court many times over four years.

Happily, in the interim, I met Elizabeth, the love of my life, and as I'll share later, we moved in together after a year. My happiness with my new love no doubt fueled some of Sylvia's rage ... the court battles were bitter and nasty. Our divorce was finalized in the spring of 1997 ... but it was a horrible, financially and emotionally draining time for everyone. Tensions between Sylvia and James and Carmen had escalated and eventually, after multiple interventions by Child Protection Services, in September 1997, the children moved in with me and Elizabeth.

After the split, all my siblings told me they were not surprised my marriage to Sylvia had failed. "After all," they said, "you married our mother." I could see that this was true. Sylvia had many of the same behaviors as Mom—minus the work ethic, minus the ability to support our family by living within our means, and minus any penchant of delayed gratification (saving money first) before purchasing something she wanted. These behaviors had created an ever-increasing debt load for us with no offsetting income to combat it.

Despite my unfortunate first marriage, as I mentioned, I did get lucky in love. I'd moved into a new life with Elizabeth, an amazing woman; eventually, she became my wife. Elizabeth is kind, generous, super smart, capable, and a hard worker (and she's still amazing!). Elizabeth's specialty is as a business strategist, facilitator, and executive coach. Her clients love her. Her collaborative strategy-building with CEOs and executive teams turns companies' financial performance from an average C to A-plus. She is responsible, accountable, knowledgeable, and sensitive, and she sees life through rose-colored glasses. She never judges anyone. If someone is being a horrible or bad person, Elizabeth will say, "He's behaving badly" ... whereas I'd say, "He's an asshole through and through." Elizabeth understands she has no insight into what is going on for that person in that moment; she doesn't know what preceded their outburst, inappropriate behavior, or remark; she doesn't know what transpired for them that day; and she doesn't know how they were raised. Her worldview was hard for me to grasp at first; however, I found it refreshing and kind. Elizabeth helped me to embrace a new life, filled with hope, promise, joy, and love—a life I had never experienced fully (other than when I was a little four year old, full of wonder and joy).

Elizabeth and I dated for about a year, then I moved into her home with her and her teenaged son, Joshua. She owned a large, two-story, four-bedroom, post-and-beam house in a good neighborhood, nestled in large, coniferous trees alongside a creek. As I mentioned earlier, in September 1997, after the third intervention of the Child Protection Services Agency, Carmen and James moved in with us. It was great for my two kids to have a new sibling to hang out with, and they got along well.

Joshua had been born in 1980 to loving parents and was raised in a nurturing, generous, caring, and understanding environment. Elizabeth and her ex-husband remained friends, and after their breakup, they focused on Joshua's welfare. Her ex was a great guy and very much a part of Joshua's life. They treated Joshua as children should be treated: with love, kindness, and respect. Although he had been an only child, Joshua became a good older brother to his two new step-siblings.

Carmen stayed with us for three years. In the third year, her behavior became obstinate, unruly, and unpredictable. It turned out that she was having greater and greater contact with her mom, Sylvia, over the phone. Sylvia was resentful and worked to drive a wedge between Carmen, Elizabeth, and me. Sylvia seemed to have a driving desire to cause me hurt and harm no matter what the cost: What was in the best interest of the children was not even a consideration.

Eventually, Sylvia succeeded. Carmen moved back in with her. That lasted less than three months, and Sylvia kicked her out. From there Carmen spent time with various other friends. Sylvia and her new husband, Willy, moved to Hamilton, Ontario. Eventually, Carmen followed and moved back in with her mom. A short while later, Carmen was out on the street. I arranged and paid for room and board so Carmen could live with a distant relative in Toronto, who was a few years her senior. When Carmen was seventeen, she told me she was pregnant and wanted to move to Texas and marry her Texan boyfriend, Bob.

To make a long story short, Carmen married Bob and had her first son just short of her eighteenth birthday. Her daughter, Lilly, was born two years later. Bob and his extended family are wonderful, loving people. Elizabeth and I remain in touch with them and our two grandkids to this day. Soon after Lilly was born, Carmen left Bob and ended up with another man whom I have not met. With this new beau, she has three daughters whom I have not met.

In January 2013, Carmen phoned me. She told me she loved me and that she would never talk to me again. She removed me and blocked me from all social media contact, email, and all other methods of communication. I have not heard from her since. So far, she has kept her word. To this day, I do not know why she did this nor do I have any contact with her.

James, on the other hand, lived with us until he finished grade twelve. He learned Spanish in high school and received excellent grades in all his courses. Creative in many areas, he learned guitar and won a weekend placement to study art with Canada's renowned naturalist and artist (painter), Robert Bateman. On graduating from grade twelve, he applied for and was accepted into two prestigious eastern Canada universities, McGill and Queen's ... in addition to being accepted simultaneously into a coveted and limited-placement organization called the Canada World Youth Program. Canada World Youth is an international non-profit organization dedicated to providing youth with a volunteer opportunity to learn about other communities, cultures, and people while developing leadership and communications skills. James deferred starting McGill University for a year to take part in the Canada World Youth opportunity. In this program, he was partnered with a Uruguayan youth, and the two of them spent three months in a rural placement in British Columbia just outside of Vernon. They were then transferred to a working farm outside of Montevideo, Uruguay for another three months. On finishing this six-month-stint, James was fully bilingual, having learned to both write and speak Spanish. The following year, he entered McGill and graduated four years later.

While in Montreal, Quebec, James became fluent in French. On graduating from McGill, he worked for two years in Montreal in a rotational management program with a well-known tech company. Since then, he has worked in various locations within Canada and in San Francisco, California. He is currently working in the financial sector with one of

Canada's largest banks. I couldn't be prouder of the man James has become. There are great things ahead for him.

With his dedication and commitment to learning and reaching his fullest potential, James reminds me a bit of me when I was a younger man. I loved learning and I knew I could do more with my life than just bounce from job to job without any real plan for my life. For example, even after I obtained my engineering degree and worked successfully for several years, I continued to pursue further education with the goal of achieving increased job responsibility and higher job satisfaction. In my mid-thirties (1995), I was debating whether to take a Master of Business Administration degree. The program was two years long, and I just could not figure out how I could work full time, do classes or homework at night and on the weekends, and do all the other things the maintenance of life requires.

Elizabeth asked me, "How long is the course?"

"Two years." I replied.

She said, "Well, the time will pass anyway, so in two years you can look back and say either, "I did it," or "I wish I had."" With Elizabeth's support and encouragement, I took the Executive Master of Business Administration (EMBA) program from Simon Fraser University, a two-year program that mid-career professionals complete while remaining in their jobs. Once I completed the course of study, I began to seek out self-help books and programs to work on improving my perspectives on life. I read books on topics such as how to change personal habits, how to become more efficient, and how to think positively, manifest my desires, become wealthy, and the like. I devoured books by Napoleon Hill, Steven Covey, Dale Carnegie, Tony Robbins, Dr. Wayne Dyer, Louise Hay, Eckhart Tolle, Jack Canfield, Mark Victor Hansen, and James Allen (to name just a few).

I attended various programs that promised to "change my life" so I could be more efficient, more productive, and happier at work. But at this point I saw the once-beloved company I worked for as an ever-increasing storm of chaotic, random decision-making. I watched some senior managers jockey for position while others tried to weather continuous political interference by the provincial owner. Over a ten-year period, the revolving door of the corner office and the constant company restructuring wore on me. While other employees seemed to manage, rolling with the changes in direction, for me, it became a bitter, toxic work environment. Other disaffected employees hung on because of the pay and the golden "handcuffs" of the defined pension plan.

I tried to change my attitude. I embraced positive thinking and covered my office walls with inspirational posters with well-known phrases to help me think differently. For example: "The art of being wise is knowing what to overlook," "Life is a tragedy for those who feel and a comedy for those who think," and "Act as if it were impossible to fail." I focused on controlling my breathing. I did my best to understand that the decisions senior management made that affected my work were their prerogative. I tried to embrace the new challenges and changing directions with a positive and hopeful attitude. On the outside, I went along with it all. But on the inside, at best, I thought they were wrong; at worst, I thought they were idiots more interested in keeping their jobs than standing up to the lunacy. It was eating me up from the inside. I judged, criticized, condemned, and demeaned. At forty-two, I had had it.

I could not take it anymore. I was stressed out and ready to go *postal* on the executives who were responsible for all the bullshit. The company's generous sick leave provision allowed me to take three months off with full pay, on short-term disability. I was under medical care, and my doctor assessed the situation and provided me with a regular, requisite note saying that "Neil is not yet able to return to work and will be re-assessed in two weeks." I forwarded that note to the company.

At the end of three month's sick leave, I had the option of applying for long-term disability (LTD). I had to either let the company know why I was off sick and apply for LTD or remain silent on the reason for my absence and go back to work. Stress leave at that time was career-limiting. I chose to remain silent.

But back at work, the company was no different. I was no different. Six months later, I quit my job. With Elizabeth's support and business contacts, I embarked on a new adventure. I started a software company with a former client of Elizabeth's. Three years later, we found ourselves under-capitalized, in a crowded technical space with an amazing piece of technology and a great client but with no further prospects against the giants that had developed and emerged over this same time period. My partner and I parted ways. He was angry and upset about how things turned out. I was not happy with the outcome either but chalked it up to a learning experience.

I went back to doing what I knew best, operating as an independent consultant project manager in the industry I knew well. Work came to me quickly and usually with only one or two phone calls. The money was good, the independence even better. We had sold the house when James was in grade eleven and moved a few kilometres away, into a sixteen-story, well-built, concrete apartment building. Our new purchase was a twelve-hundred-square-foot apartment that had two bedrooms and two bathrooms. Joshua moved out into a rental home with a group of his friends. As mentioned previously, James left a year after graduating from grade twelve to attend university in Montreal.

Elizabeth's dream had been to live on the Sunshine Coast, and in 2007, we purchased a waterfront lot in Pender Harbour, a forty-minute ferry ride and two-hour car ride away. We designed and built our dream house and sold our condominium in town. We were empty nesters, and our children were launched.

Our Pender Harbour home was—and still is—a masterpiece, with the best finishes we could afford, built by a reputable builder known for high-end homes. It was costly. We joked to ourselves that this would be either the best or worst financial decision we ever made, and we believed we couldn't possibly go wrong. After all, the Vancouver and surrounding real estate market for the past ten years had just kept climbing in value at an unprecedented pace. The market was known worldwide, sought after for its location, beauty, and lifestyle value. We laid down our bet. We thought it would be a sound investment—beautiful oceanfront property with unparalleled views, in an idyllic, remote wilderness—all within three to four hours from Vancouver.

Of course, the 2008 crash caused a momentary slowdown of the Vancouver real estate market, but it re-surged and now remains on course, with record growth and no end in sight. The Sunshine Coast market, however, crashed heavily and never recovered. Our new home was amazing, peaceful, and personally restorative to mind and body. It was an oasis of beauty, joy, and tranquility, but to maintain the business, the house, the travel, the lifestyle, and the associated second home costs required an annual $300K income just to break even. In addition, all our clients were in Vancouver and the surrounding metropolitan area. The one-way trip to and from the city (with waiting time for the ferry and traffic conditions) took roughly three to four hours, so we had to stay in hotels every two weeks or rent an apartment so we could service our clients properly. The cost of a hotel versus a one-bedroom, one-bathroom apartment was comparable. We vacillated between staying at hotels and renting an apartment. They each had their advantages and disadvantages. In the end, we stayed at hotels for a couple of years, then we opted to rent a one-bedroom apartment.

Elizabeth had steady client work she loved, while my work with my clients was slowing down. Instead of looking for more work in a field where I could do "what I do best," I decided I wanted a change. I let the project management work end and embarked on a new venture. I had illusions of wealth and grandeur. Elizabeth refers to this next three-year period as *the time I sunk into madness*. I can see clearly now that she was right.

I went into a business I had no business being in. It was an exercise in self-delusion and futility. Over those three years, my lack of income drained our entire savings and brought us to the brink of bankruptcy. We put the house up for sale, but the market had fallen so low that we would easily lose seven figures and have neither a home nor savings to show for a lifetime of work. I managed to right myself on the work front and secured a long-term contract doing "what I do best." This stemmed the monthly losses, but that was all. We knew we would still have to sell the house.

It was a weird time in our lives. We worked hard serving our clients and enjoyed work satisfaction and success. The Pender Harbour home was a peaceful respite surrounded by wildlife that became part of our daily lives; deer, coyotes, a bear (we called her Elsie), a plethora of bald eagles, turkey vultures, woodpeckers, ravens, and a fabulous murder of crows we called Benny and the Jets. Sunrises, sunsets, and end-to-end vistas of rainbows graced us with their beauty, but the financial burden of maintaining both the house and a rented apartment, plus biweekly travel was mentally, emotionally, and physically draining.

Even though in the following pages I am going to continue to share my woes, life circumstances, and the thinking that drove me to write that suicide note at the kitchen table, I want you to know that there were many good experiences in my life as well. For example, both Elizabeth and I love to travel. We love art and architecture. As such, here's a partial list of the places we visited between 1995 and 2017: Toronto, Montreal, New York City (four times), San Francisco, Las Vegas, Florida, Texas, Hawaii, Alaska, and Australia. Our favourite adventure (always) was Europe. We took about fifteen trips to Europe, traveling through France, Germany, Luxembourg, Austria, and Italy. For Elizabeth's sixty-fifth birthday, we took Joshua and James to Venice; it was a great family holiday. We visited Elizabeth's German relatives in towns and cities throughout Germany. It was always magical, always fun ... and always for at least three weeks at a time. We traveled on points. Even though a limited budget kept us tucked firmly into business or economy class, once we even traveled first class. If you ever experience international first class, you won't want to go back. We have memories that will never fade with time!

Because I am an enthusiastic BMW motorcyclist, Elizabeth suggested I enjoy a trip on my own. I flew nonstop, first-class on a Lufthansa Airlines round trip to Munich and spent two glorious weeks on an organized Classic Alpine tour with Beach's Motorcycle Adventures (https://www.bmca.com). The owners, Rob and Gretchen Beach, provide a first-class experience with a plethora of pre-planned daily routes to choose from. I consider them friends for life after one tour. You can read more about this trip in the Appendix – "My Incredible Motorcycling Alpine Adventure."

Unfortunately for me, the good times did not win over the negative, self-destructive thought patterns that created my daily life experiences. So, back to my story of my self-created hell on earth....

For me, day-to-day life was both heaven on earth and hell at the same time. But my dire attitude, negative behavior, constant doom and gloom, and emotional outbursts were wearing Elizabeth down. The constant stress ramped up my fears, anxieties, and phobias. The OCD was prevalent in all my activities—and it was getting worse. These conditions and behaviors created additional stresses, both for Elizabeth and for our relationship.

I saw no positive outcomes in our future. No savings, no one interested in buying the house, no increase in market value, constant commuting, constant costs, endless client work just to stay afloat. On top of all that, in July 2017, I developed a medical condition that threatened to limit my ability to drive, to work on a computer, or to be outside in the open air. In other words, it threatened to change my life drastically and even possibly eliminate my ability to work and earn an income. I felt we were hooped. I was the cause; it was all my fault. Fifty-seven. Useless. A burden financially and physically to Elizabeth and our family. The medical practitioners held no hope for recovery; they told me it was just something I would have to learn to live with.

The only future I could imagine was losing the house, owing the bank the shortfalls of a forfeit sale, and being out on the street with nowhere to go and no money. Elizabeth kept telling me, "We will be fine." I believed she was being unrealistically optimistic, looking through those rose-colored glasses of hers; with no appreciation for reality.

Deep depression set in. I hid all kinds of emotions and never shared these feelings with anyone for fear of being judged. I lied and pretended everything was okay. Elizabeth never knew. She only knew that my phobias and OCD were out of control.

I started to listen to audiobooks … self-help spiritual books … science-based books … I even read an autobiographical account of a near-death experience (NDE) by Anita Moorjani. The spiritual books held promise and the possibility of a solution. Some even offered hope for healing and full recovery from all of life's ills and provided methods or a process to follow. But absolutely none of these methods or processes had worked for me in the past. They all required a wholesale change in thoughts and beliefs, combined with superhuman willpower. I knew it was going to be no different this time. The scientific, fact-based books offered hope, but none provided any real or tangible methods or processes to create the healing I so desperately needed.

Moorjani's autobiography did, however, offer a new type of hope … a clear, profoundly inspiring description of the beautiful origin of life … where we come from and the beautiful existence to which we will return. Even though Moorjani experienced a truly remarkable, scientifically documented, complete, absolute (though medically unexplainable) healing of a terminal illness, it was unlikely that my condition would result in the same comatose near-death experience. Moorjani describes for her readers a beautiful end state, but she does not offer a process or method for healing. She did bring back messages that say we are not judged or punished for what we do in our lives. Great news, of course, but still—no method, and no tangible hope for healing my thoughts, my beliefs, or my body.

Then, two things happened. First, the house had been on the market for over six years with no bites. In September, we dropped the asking price again and in late October, we received an offer that we accepted—reluctantly. It was better to sell and lift the ever-increasing financial weight from our shoulders than to hang on and hope for a better offer. If the buyer's conditions were removed, and the sale was finalized, we could be free of debt. In early November, the subjects were removed and the sale went through. With this news, Elizabeth left for Toronto in early November 2017 to visit with her brother and his family.

I was alone in our one-bedroom rental apartment. I was sick and tired of being sick and tired. There seemed to be no way out. Why on earth would I endure another year? Let alone twenty or thirty more years? The deep, prolonged depression and feelings of hopelessness had dashed my dreams. I was at the end of my rope. This was my chance—I could free myself from the endless burdens of life and let Elizabeth live in peace and financial security with the payout of my life insurance.

As I said earlier, the messages highlighted in Moorjani's book had alleviated my nagging Christian doubt and fear—there would be no retribution, no damnation to hell, no judgment or punishment if I committed the grievous act. I had permission to do it. So, alone at the kitchen table, I planned and wrote my suicide note. I could make up for the pain, worry, stress, and distress I had caused Elizabeth at last. She would be burdened no more.

Coincidentally, though, something had happened just before Elizabeth left for Toronto that shone a glimmer of hope into my desperate life. I came across a new manuscript, a set of "Letters," that inspired me to study one last "set of Truths"—Truths that promised to liberate me. "Suicide will always be an option," I thought. Deep down it felt wrong. "I'll give it one last chance," I decided. I put the suicide note in a safe place, set a timeline, and began to study.

Well, as you can tell, the information and new knowledge I gained saved my life. The manuscript promised to set me on a path to revitalize my life—and it worked. It can work for you too. I hope you'll read on and complete the exercises and program of study I offer in the following sections. Included in Part III is the first step in the seven-step process I followed to freedom. It was through following these seven simple steps that I learned the lessons that changed my life. With effort, determination, and dedication, you too can use this process to transform your life.

Part III prepares you to better comprehend the "Truths" through the use of new scientific discoveries in bioenergetics, epigenetics, and human development. The scientific teachings will open your mind so you can have the optimum chance of understanding the knowledge shared in Part IV. As I noted in Chapter One, Part III ends with a glimpse—a sliver of a vision, of what happens to you after the death of the body, of where you come from, and where you go. I have drawn this vision from Anita Moorjani's account of the NDE she describes in vivid detail in her book *Dying to Be Me*. You'll need to read her account so that you too can expand your current thinking and imagine vividly the Truth of your reality.

None of the information I am about to share comes from me. I am merely an instrument to introduce you to and guide you through the process, helping to ensure your success and the best possible outcome.

To that end, I implore you: *Follow my steps*. As mentioned in the Preface, read this book cover to cover and you will understand the process in its entirety. Then come back and do the required work, starting with Step One. (Alternatively, you may begin with one or more of the suggested scientific readings discussed in the next chapter, prior to starting Step One.)

After you begin with Step One, follow the *Seven Steps* in sequential order. Do not skip ahead or ignore a directed reading or exercise. If you complete the steps in the order given, you will have the best chance of digesting these learnings—and understanding them clearly will enable you to change your life's circumstances. I assure you, there is no more simple way to change your life, but you need to be dedicated, determined, and patient.

Let's begin....

PART III

OPENING YOUR MIND

A man's mind may be likened to a garden, which may be intelligently cultivated or allowed to run wild; but whether cultivated or neglected, it must, and will, bring forth. If no useful seeds are put into it, then an abundance of useless weed seeds will fall therein, and will continue to produce their kind.[9]

—James Allen

Chapter 6

SCIENCE AND A NEW VISION

Every human being's essential nature is perfect and
faultless, but after years of immersion in the world we
easily forget our roots and take on a counterfeit nature.[10]

—Lao Tzu

Vancouver's Pacific National Exhibition (PNE) is held the last two
weeks of August and ends on Labor Day Monday. It is a typical
fair: midway rides and food, agricultural exhibits and contests,
horse races and dog shows, music and concerts. It includes one
large building stuffed with exhibitors in small booths peddling a
variety of gadgets: kitchen knives, magic cleaning cloths, vacuum
cleaners, women's beauty products, jewelry, household products,
and so on.

For me, a highlight of the fair is the PNE Lottery. At each of
the multiple points of entry, visitors are greeted by the familiar

cry of "Win a house! Win a car!" Throughout my childhood, each year, my mother would go immediately to one of these purveyors of possible fortune and purchase a bank of tickets. They came on sheets of paper—five, ten, or twenty tickets with the price per ticket decreasing for each increasing lot size. Mom always purchased one or two of the twenty-ticket lots.

The tickets were small, and there were perforations between each ticket for easy separation. Each ticket had to be filled in by hand in pen or pencil: name, address, phone number. Then they would be torn apart on the perforation and deposited in one of the wooden boxes near the sellers' booths. This was an annual ritual. The potential winnings included cars of various models and a grand prize of a pre-built, fully furnished house, in a new development somewhere in B.C. The house was assembled on the PNE grounds for viewing by prospective winners. Every year, we stood in line to tour the house and see what we would—hopefully—be winning.

Mom never won.

I caught the Prize Home bug, and from the age of twenty onwards, I bought lottery tickets at the fair annually. I purchased the tickets, crossed my fingers for a win, and then never gave it a second thought. My desire was to win the house. I never really paid attention to the lineup of cars; I already had a nice car—it was the house I wanted. (Fortunately, tickets can now be purchased online. Win or lose, the funds raise support for PNE operations, which I consider a worthy cause.)

In 2010, my dream car was a silver Lexus hardtop convertible. In September 2010, I cut out a picture of it and posted it on a bulletin board in my office. Sitting quietly in my office chair, I would look at the picture and capture the image in my mind. Closing my eyes, I would take a few minutes and imagine myself driving that car, grin on my face, feeling joy in my heart and the wind in my hair as I navigated the twisting, coastal road up to Pender Harbour. I felt the pride of ownership. I did this about fifteen to twenty times a day, every day, for about a year.

In May 2011, PNE Lottery tickets became available online. I bought one hundred dollars' worth; these included a variety of Early Bird draws. "Win a house! Win a car!" As previously mentioned, I paid no attention to the types of cars available that year—my hope, as always, was on winning the house. September 5 was the draw for the house, and they phoned the winner while broadcasting live on TV. I had forgotten all about it and did not receive that call.

On September 8, I received a call from caller ID: "PNE." A pleasant woman greeted me and verified my name. "You've won a car in the PNE lottery," she said.

"A car! What kind of car?" I asked.

"A silver Lexus IS350C," she replied.

"What kind of Lexus is that?" I asked.

"A hardtop convertible," she said.

I had won my dream car. "Wow," I thought to myself, "how lucky!" And yes, it was a very nice ride indeed.

In this book, I share the principles and mechanisms I unknowingly put into action that manifested my dream car. But my purpose in sharing this process *goes beyond helping you to draw everything you desire into your life*. I want to help you *free yourself from that ever-turning treadmill* that bears you continually into circumstances you do not enjoy.

To break free of that treadmill, to attain your true purpose in life, it is important to understand your true origins and the principles and processes outlined later in this book. These principles and process I call *Truths*. Once you fully understand these Truths and put them into daily practice, you will be able to step off the treadmill. In this book, I'll share with you a "shortcut"—a more streamlined process than the one I followed. I have shared this "condensed version" with a friend, who confirms that the process outlined on the following pages is vital to opening your mind to receive and comprehend the Truths presented in Part IV of this book.

The process summarized is similar to learning to become a master painter. As a new artist, first, you learn the fundamentals of painting—how to mix colors; what types of brushes to use. Next, you might create an underlying drawing that you fill in with color. As you practice and learn, you become aware of the artful use of color and the relationships of shape in things you are looking at. Later, you use your new awareness to inform and enrich your work. With practice and continued instruction, you build on your foundation and eventually become a master.

The process on the following pages will help you build a solid foundation—first, you'll open your mind; then, you'll learn new, specific information and instructions for daily practice. With time, patience, dedication, and daily work, eventually, you will become a master: master of your life, master of your fate, master of your destiny.

You know from reading this book so far that I accumulated a lifetime of beliefs and thoughts that brought me to the brink of suicide. I have read hundreds of self-help books and articles over the years in an attempt to manifest my dreams of generating prosperity and finding peace in my life. For example, I worked to change my thinking by following methods of positive thinking and eliminating negative thinking. I practiced being more grateful and controlling my emotions. While all the material I studied identified the self-limiting beliefs I held, and provided processes to change them, I was never successful at shifting my fundamental, ingrained (and many false) beliefs about life and about myself. Reasons and excuses always got in the way: my genetics, my family of origin, my childhood learnings and experiences, my middle-class station in life, my rightness. These beliefs were cemented within me. They were either facts of immutable biology and makeup, facts of physical existence ... or they were my parents' fault. Or so I believed.

For my entire life, right up until seven months after I began this process, my nights were dominated by fearful, sad, disturbing dreams, or hours of sleeplessness. Lying awake, I was consumed by grief and anxiety. Asleep or awake, I focused on everything negative and scary: worry about our financial situation or about things that happened or might happen; feeling angry or frustrated about work or my personal interactions with people. Other sources of anxiety included disturbing things I had heard, read, or seen on the news, in movies, on TV, or in a book I was reading before I drifted off to sleep. I woke up each morning disturbed and grumpy. Of course, this affected my interactions with my wife and others during the day. Conversely, when I awoke from a restful night, I was pleasant and on top of the world. This may have lasted all day, or may have been quickly torpedoed by a negative experience or interaction with someone. Only through sheer willpower could I rise above those daily ups-and-downs and maintain a happy demeanor on a regular basis.

I know now that in order to be successful in transforming your life, you cannot do it using willpower alone. All of the methods I tried previously: thinking positively, eliminating negative thinking, being grateful, being mindful, controlling my emotions, and writing down and visualizing clear goals and outcomes all required a continuous, conscious effort of willpower. These methods proved transient / temporary (and likely will not work for most people) because it was a battle of wills: willpower versus ego. I struggled relentlessly to adopt a more loving way of thinking, feeling, and responding to every experience, but while I (my willpower) remained the single motivating force within my consciousness, eventually, my ego won, taking me back to my starting point. I was never successful at attaining a wholesale change in my thinking or emotions. All the things I wanted, yearned for, and hoped for eluded me.

In the rest of this book, I offer you a method of cleansing your consciousness to achieve true peace, joy, abundance, and prosperity and a method of embodying and expressing unconditional love. Feeling grateful, thinking positively, and being emotionally uplifted into an inner state of peace and love are all corresponding outcomes. You don't have to try to do or be these things; they just happen. Let's now begin this journey and learn how to achieve the lasting rewards of personal fulfilment and happiness for you.

Have you ever noticed how a change in thought can change how you are feeling instantly? One minute, you are happy and enjoying life, then someone says something or you receive an email or text with upsetting news. Your body and your emotions react. You become sad, angry, frustrated, or just plain pissed off—all because a thought, a suggestion, a piece of news, or something you witnessed upset you. You can go quickly from being happy to sad to being angry or frustrated, but it is not as easy to go from being sad, angry, or frustrated to being happy.

Most people will agree that a daily diet of healthy, life-giving nutrition is important for your overall health and wellbeing. I now believe that your "mental diet" is even more important. Take a moment and think about what you feed your mind every minute of every day. Radio, TV, movies, newspapers, books, magazines, news alerts on your electronic devices ... all chock-a-block full of negative stories: economic crises; climate change; wars; unbridled violence; promiscuous, emotionally superficial sex; greed; suffering; racism ... to name just a few. This mental diet and its effects on you are amplified by the accompanying explicit images and scenes portrayed in movies, TV, and in other media. With daily consumption over a long period, imperceptibly and insidiously, this mental diet alters your mental makeup (thoughts and feelings) subliminally. These changes happen so slowly, you do not notice them. New consciousness patterns and thought forms with corresponding emotions become your new norm. When a majority of people consume the same type of mental food, the norms of society change.

This mental diet objectifies women, men, and the human race in general. It desensitizes us (and our societies) to these denigrating, disturbing, and destructive creations of consciousness, and they are carried into our lives and actions. These changes include the evolution of social mores. For example, subject matter that was deemed unacceptable in film and media in the 1950s is acceptable today. Similarly, just seventy years ago, it would have been inconceivable to discuss certain content publicly or to depict it in images—now that same content is readily available on the internet with just a few keystrokes on your computer.

Think about the types of things depicted in entertainment that are consumed daily by a majority of people. If what is shown in entertainment were to materialize in our real lives, surely this would be cause for concern. As it says in the material referenced in the next chapter:

> ...[I]f you reflect honestly on conditions in your present lives, you will realize that they are becoming a terror-inducing mirror image of all that your entertainment industry has given you in the past [70] years. ... Why? Because your so-called civilized 'culture' permits brutality in all its perverted forms, to enter your homes through the medium of your TV... [the internet, and other media] for your titillation and excitement.[11]

Unknowingly, we have altered our individual and collective consciousness, thereby creating our current reality.

To change our current collective reality, first we must each change ourselves. Slowly, as more and more people perceive the difference between wholesome, life-giving consciousness forms—thoughts, emotions, words, and deeds—and destructive consciousness patterns, through our new demeanor and actions, we will inspire others to do the same. Over time, as more and more people realize and accept this truth, the collective consciousness will change. These changes will uplift the collective consciousness. In turn, we will save humankind and our planet from our current path of self-driven annihilation. Can you imagine how wonderful that will be?

I'm not suggesting you stick your head in the sand or turn a blind eye to what is going on in the world around you. However, it is important that you are aware of the mental diet you consume every day and its impact on your consciousness. Your mental diet permeates your mind. The images, language, and behaviors you feed on influence your thoughts and emotional reactions. In turn, these are linked strongly to your feelings and become embedded in your subconscious mind. These fixed, recurring thoughts affect your mental and emotional makeup and, over time, they result in unintentional, habitual thoughts, judgments, behaviors, and actions. Once these thoughts are imprinted emotionally in your subconscious mind, they become conditioned thoughts and behaviors and, like concrete, they are very hard to break.

The ever-powerful subconscious mind controls our belief systems, what we think of ourselves, and how we see the world and our place in it. It becomes our self-image, it dictates the lifestyle we think we deserve, and it determines what we think we can (and cannot) do. It will express itself uncontrollably when a stimulus triggers a conditioned response. As noted earlier, your mental diet affects your thinking and emotions, and what is in your mind will create all your future experiences, be it an experience that happens a few moments from now or days, weeks, months, or years from now. The process and teachings offered in this book will empower you, as an individual, to improve your life through understanding the truth of your origins, what your creative tools are, and how you create your every experience through your thoughts and emotions. And most importantly, the teachings will show how you can transform your life for the better. It is my hope that as more people start to live their ideal lives of love, peace, and joy, the world will begin to evolve and change for the better. If you've read this far, I think that's what you want too. Together let's make it happen...

HOW TO CHANGE YOUR WORLD TO ONE OF LOVE, PEACE, AND JOY

In this section, first we define a common language and explore the concept of consciousness, and then we move into the realm of science. Provided in the Science section are four outlines of science-based books I recommend you read and one outline of a book about an author's personal near-death experience (NDE) that I consider a vital *must-read* in opening your mind to consider a new concept of our origins. Please read this NDE experiencer's book—it is Step One of the *Seven Steps* offered in this book to help you transform your life.

The section on consciousness offers you my view of consciousness and lays the groundwork for the new concepts presented to you in the science-based books. These books begin the process of opening your mind and preparing you for a radical shift in understanding your origins and the mechanisms that, unknowingly, you use to shape your life. These readings will prepare you to transform your life and circumstances dramatically. I am *introducing* you to the four science-based books and suggest you read them. I am not providing an executive summary of them or a dissertation on them. If the concepts presented are new to you, these books will be important for you to read in the journey to opening your mind and broadening your perspectives of our current reality.

As noted earlier, I recommend you approach these *Seven Steps* in a precise, step-by-step progression:

- Read this book from cover to cover (in order to attain a high-level overview of the Steps).
- Then, come back to begin the process to change your life, and either:
  ○ read one or more of the scientific books before moving onto Step One, or
  ○ start directly working with Step One.

You may wonder why I did not provide a Coles Notes version of these authors' works, in order to make your life simpler. Well, a summary of their work would be insufficient, and perhaps misleading, and, in my view, would not be in your best interest overall. I believe firmly that you must comprehend and digest these authors' findings personally. My goal is to prepare you to be as open-minded as possible by the time you get to Step Two of this book. So, please, if the scientific readings are new to you, take the time to read them before proceeding to Step One. If you are already familiar with them, then start with Step One. As I mentioned before, your consciousness evolution is not a quick fix; it takes work and dedication. But I guarantee it will be worth every moment you spend in proper preparation. I promise.

First, we delve into the concept of consciousness. Then, we explore what science can tell us. Then, by stressing a particular personal experience of Anita Moorjani's, I hope to broaden and stretch your understanding of life and give you a glimpse of what your future can hold. Furthermore, imagination alone can soar no further than your previous experiences; your personal frame of reference. Therefore, you are confined to your past, which you project into your future. To help you break free of the confines of your past that project you unchanged into your future, it is important that you consider new concepts—and Anita's personal account of what happens after we die is an ideal, life-affirming, and life-transforming illustration of what lies ahead for each of us.

To help you break free from the confines of your past that project you unchanged into your future, it is important that you consider new concepts about yourself, life, and consciousness.

It helps to have a common language when walking a common path. Following are definitions from the www.lexico.com *UK Dictionary* of five words that will be used throughout the rest of this book: Mind, Brain, Consciousness, Emotion, and Belief.

Mind:	*The element of a person that enables them to be aware of the world and their experiences; to think, and to feel; the faculty of consciousness and thought.*[12]
Brain:	*An organ of soft nervous tissue contained in the skull of vertebrates, functioning as the coordinating centre of sensation and intellectual and nervous activity.*[13]
Consciousness:	*The state of being aware of and responsive to one's surroundings. A person's awareness or perception of something. The fact of awareness by the mind of itself and the world.*[14]
Emotion:	*A strong feeling deriving from one's circumstances, mood, or relationships with others. Instinctive or intuitive feeling as distinguished from reasoning or knowledge.*[15]

Belief:	*An acceptance that something exists or is true, especially one without proof. Something one accepts as true or real; a firmly held opinion. Trust, faith, or confidence in (someone or something).*[16]

What is Consciousness?

Have you ever stopped to think about consciousness? About where your thoughts come from and where they are stored? I thought for many years that all my thoughts originated from my brain. I thought my brain was a great warehouse of everything I had ever read, heard, or experienced. I believed my thoughts consisted of data pulled from the warehouse and cobbled together in a logical (and sometimes illogical) pattern of things, then expressed in words that were consistent with those learnings; those beliefs. As I grew older and experienced a few lapses of memory, I believed it was not because the information had disappeared but rather because I could not access it in that moment. Perhaps the neural pathways had too much information to sift through quickly. Or maybe there was just so much information clogging up the neural pathways that my ability to recall and retrieve the stored information in a timely manner, from that library-sized warehouse, was temporarily impeded or blocked.

Today I have an entirely new concept of consciousness, thoughts, beliefs, and truth. I now see my thinking more as a stream of thoughts, endless in nature, unlimited in permutation, that flow by and into my awareness constantly. I no longer see them as self-generated but instead as a stream of consciousness from outside me that I observe, contemplate, and choose. What I choose is influenced by my beliefs, by my subconscious programming, by my emotional imprints, and by how open I am (or am not) to considering new perspectives and ideas. What I choose to think is entirely up to me! I can select a thought, contemplate it—and then choose to keep it or throw it back into the stream. This process happens in a nanosecond. I can accept and keep a thought, or throw it back easily and quickly.

My mental diet feeds this stream and can be healthy and life-giving or can pollute it. If my mental diet is permeated with loving, generous thoughts and behaviors, my stream remains predominantly pure. If my mental diet is permeated with greed and self-interest, with violence witnessed personally or depicted in the entertainment and news I watch, my stream becomes more and more toxic and the relative volume of loving and generous thoughts are near impossible to contemplate or choose. Instead, I end up choosing and reinforcing contaminated, life-harming thoughts.

In the past, prior to 2017, when I was less discerning about issues regarding my mental diet, I would explore things on the internet. Whenever I was surveying social media platforms (YouTube, for example), I would watch one video ... that would lead me to another video ... and so on. Inevitably, I would end up down what some clever web writer referred to as *the internet rabbit hole* ... only to wake up three to four hours later in what that astute writer called *a dissociative, fugue-like state* ... with no idea of where the time went and no memory of the mental smorgasbord of shiny, pre-packaged things I had just consumed. Have you experienced a similar event? It is easy to do when we are not consciously aware of what we are exposing ourselves to and the dangerous effect it can have on our thoughts, emotions, and beliefs.

Similarly, your stream of thoughts and what you choose to think drives your life, influences your experiences, and affects your health in a life-giving, healthy way ... or not.

Let's explore what science says on the topic of both your mental diet and how your thoughts affect your life and your biology.

Science

The scientific fraternity (and the established institutions that house it) is steeped in traditions of reason and logic. Scientific findings, to be credible to other scientists, must be observable, measurable, calculable, and proven by instruments. Since the time of Darwin, science has brought us new insights into the mechanics and evolution of life and biology. Technologically based science has brought humanity many conveniences to make our lives easier and safer.

These advances have both positive and negative consequences. They make our lives more convenient and our medical treatments more effective, but when driven by human greed and self-interest, they can create irreversible environmental damage and pollution, the extinction of species, and (potentially) the annihilation of our planet.

As an engineer, I was schooled in reason, logic, measurement, and observation, the process for all scientific and traditional academic schooling and research. The following four scientific books follow these same scientific principles. Before I introduce you to them, however, I want to point out that science tells us our universe is composed of energy particles. All matter is really energy particles bonded together in various patterns to form what we see as solid. Even organic matter, plants, humans, and animals are comprised, subatomically, of energy particles. So, what we see as solid is really not solid at all. You know this fact intellectually. But for most people it has not yet filtered through (even remotely) to their consciousness to give them a new perspective on the world and existence itself. Believe it or not, your thinking affects the vibration of these energy particles, either speeding them up or slowing them down. If you can suspend any disbelief about this notion momentarily, and carry it with you as you explore the scientific books I have recommended, you will begin to change your perspective on the world and existence.

Please note: If you choose to download audiobooks for learning this material, I recommend you do the following:

Tips for Listening to an Audiobook

1. Because of the nature and content of the books, the material requires careful listening ... listening that is not distracted by other activities.
2. I suggest you:
   - find a comfortable chair (I use a recliner).
   - sit in a relaxed position, as if you were about to pick up a print copy book.
   - use headphones.
   - close your eyes and listen to the book.

The reason I make these suggestions is that in order for you to absorb fully what is being said and really understand all the principles being taught, you need to be focused on the task, and not be visually distracted or preoccupied by doing chores, driving your car, or walking. In addition, in the next chapter, I will share a specific meditation that requires that you still your mind. You will need to focus your mind—on nothing. This requires concentration.

Like most people, I am a visual learner. However, out of necessity, in 2017, I needed to master learning by listening to audio recordings. The tips I suggest above helped me learn how to concentrate on the spoken word without being visually distracted. (As my wife will tell you, I can be distracted easily.) Without knowing it at that time, the tips above helped me train my mind and concentrate my focus. The unintended consequence was that I learned the specific meditation technique and how to execute it effectively to achieve optimum results.

Let's now begin with the concept of the influence and effect of memes on individuals and society.

Mind and Memes

Recommended Read: *Virus of the Mind* by Richard Brodie[17]/[18] Richard Brodie's book *Virus of the Mind* is about the science of memes, also referred to as "memetics." Brodie explores how memes influence our lives, building on the work of other scientists interested in memes and their potential impact on people and societies.[19]

The term "meme" was coined in 1976 by the evolutionary biologist Richard Dawkins in his seminal work, *The Selfish Gene.*[20] Memetics is the study of the workings of memes; how they penetrate, copy, instruct, and spread. Just like a biological virus that penetrates a human cell, injects instructions, piggybacks on that cell's replication processes, spreads within the host, and uses its host's biological responses (such as coughing or sneezing) to spread and infect others, a meme spreads from mind to mind through interactions of consciousness.

A meme has no physical properties. It is a thought, a belief, an attitude that spreads from one person to another. Once it infects you, it influences your thinking. Once it embeds itself in your thoughts, your emotions cement it into your subconsciousness. We are all infected with various memes. Memes are passed down through the ages by grandparents to parents to children; they are passed from one person to another through conversations, media, books, TV, and now through various internet highways, including social media sites. Truths and mistruths fill the internet arena these days, and they travel globally at an unprecedented rate. With no real thought, we pass them on for others to consume and digest, and others are affected by them unknowingly. They spread like wildfire and impact the so-called "collective consciousness." You can see from reading my personal history the various memes I adopted that affected my thinking (mind), emotions, actions, and eventually, my body (biology). After reading *Virus of the Mind*, you too may want to consider how these non-physical entities are affecting how you think, feel, and behave.

Brodie's book is an important read that will introduce you to how human beings spread these mental viruses knowingly, unknowingly, and deliberately through designer memes. We spread them easily because of our readily available communication highways. These mental viruses have become a portion of our mental diet and are having a significant impact, both on individuals and on societies. They are surreptitiously shaping our cultural evolution—and not necessarily for the better.

Most importantly, they can affect your biology. The next reading explains how.

Mind and Cells

Recommended Read: *The Biology of Belief* by Bruce H. Lipton[21] Bruce H. Lipton is a cell biologist and former medical school professor. Lipton quit his teaching position when he realized that his research results consistently contradicted what he was required to teach his medical students. Lipton explains in easy-to-understand language that genes and DNA do not control our biology. Instead, his (and others') research shows that our cells are controlled mainly by signals from outside of the cells. These signals come from our thoughts. In short, the way we think and what we believe controls our biology—and our biological outcomes.

Our bodies are made up of over fifty trillion single cells. The only difference between a liver cell and a kidney cell is the work they do. Lipton says, "...the character of our lives is determined not by our genes but by our responses to the environmental signals that propel life."[22] He goes on to say that "The belief that we are frail, biochemical machines controlled by genes is giving way to an understanding that we are powerful creators of our lives and the world in which we live."[23] Lipton reports that you can change your biology, your genetic structure, and your physical makeup by changing your beliefs, your perceptions, and your thoughts.

This book will show you how cells and the work they do are influenced by their environment. You'll discover that your thoughts and emotions—positive and negative—affect and influence a cell's genetic expression (the work that a cell does). Your thoughts and emotions express electromagnetic energy waves. These energy waves affect and change your cellular biology. The resulting changes in cellular biology can either be beneficial to your makeup or can cause you harm. In short, your thinking and emotions have the power to alter your physical makeup. Dr. Lipton's book is an important read—it will expand your thinking and open your mind to new concepts about consciousness and about how your thoughts and emotions impact your biology and your life. His interesting, easy-to-read explanation of the science of epigenetics will also help to change your beliefs and attitudes regarding genetic determinism—that is, the idea that our genes are fixed, immutable, and outside of our conscious control.

The next two books I recommend that you read discuss how our thoughts can deliberately (and physically) alter our brains. I urge you read at least one of these two books, if not both. They deal with the scientific concepts of neuroplasticity and neurogenesis (in ordinary language: the idea that the brain has a profound ability to change). The first book is by the late Sharon Begley, senior science writer at Boston Globe Media's STAT. The second book is by author and psychiatrist Dr. Norman Doidge. If you know and understand that neuroplasticity and neurogenesis are both scientifically proven facts, then Doidge's book may be a good choice for you. Begley's book is a rather technical read on the medical science and research that uncovered these abilities of the brain. A short summary of both books follows.

Mind and Brain

Recommended Read: *Train Your Mind, Change Your Brain* by Sharon Begley[24]

The late Sharon Begley was a senior science writer who focused her work on medical science and research. *Train Your Mind, Change Your Brain* is a story of how researchers uncovered the brain's ability to change, even in adults. This is not a how-to book, and it is the most technical of the books I am recommending. If you find it too dry or too technical, I suggest you read *at it* over time.

Begley's book lays out, in a clear, logical, and extensive fashion, the new way scientists think about neuroplasticity and neurogenesis. It opens with a brief foreword and backdrop of discussions with His Holiness the 14th Dalai Lama. A key insight of Buddhist philosophy is that one can, by meditation and other techniques, change the way one's mind works. As with other ingrained scientific beliefs, neuroplasticity and neurogenesis were long derided by scientists. Now, the belief that we can change our brain has growing support from neuroscience research. Here's what Begley says about the power of the brain to change, not through prescription drugs but through will: "The conscious act of thinking about one's thoughts in a different way changes the very brain circuits that do that thinking..."[25] and "The ability of thought and attention to physically alter the brain echoes one of Buddhism's more remarkable hypotheses: that will is a real, physical force that can change the brain."[26] This is an important discovery for science and humankind because it suggests that recovery from a debilitating event (like a stroke or other brain trauma), from Obsessive Compulsive Disorder (OCD), or from depression is possible.

This book is an important read that will introduce you to how your thoughts can influence, affect, and change your brain and its makeup. It (as well as the suggested alternative book by Norman Doidge (see next summary)) provides insightful, promising, and mind-altering information to help prepare you for the information you will be introduced to later in this book.

As mentioned previously, if Begley's book is too technical or not of interest because of the depth of scientific research discussed, I offer you the following easier, engaging read.

Recommended Read: *The Brain That Changes Itself* by Norman Doidge, M.D.[27]

Dr. Norman Doidge is a psychiatrist, psychoanalyst, and researcher. In this book, he explores ground-breaking research in neuroplasticity through the sharing of fascinating stories of people who used their brains' abilities to adapt and be cured of ailments previously thought incurable. His examples are emotionally engaging, sometimes heart-wrenching, and in the end, uplifting. It is a fascinating read that will astound you: The human brain is incredible! Whereas formerly it was thought that the brain is hard-wired, and unchangeable, and that it declines in ability as we age, the science of neuroplasticity has proven these assumptions false. Doidge teaches us about the wonders of neuroplasticity in a way that we (non-neuroscientists) can understand. This book will empower you by helping you realize that you can change and improve your brain throughout your life, even in late adulthood.

Before proceeding to Step One, let's review briefly a science-based article on near-death experiences (NDEs)—"Near-Death Experiences, Evidence for Their Reality."[28] This eight-page article is an interesting, informative read—especially for those who are skeptical. The article, written by Dr. Jeffrey Long, appeared in *Missouri Medicine* (the Journal of the Missouri State

Medical Association). Dr. Long "...is a radiation oncologist in Houma, Louisiana and a recognized world expert on near-death experiences. Dr. Long established the nonprofit Near Death Experience Research Foundation and a website forum (*www.nderf.org*) for people to share their NDEs."[29] The article discusses the results of a large-scale study of NDEs. The study encompassed over 3,700 accounts of NDEs from around the world. The paper presents the methodology, provides examples of participants' stories, and summarizes statistics about each of nine postulated lines of evidence explored. The final statistic (outside of the nine lines of evidence explored) shares the results of an independent survey of 1,122 "NDErs" who were asked: "How do you currently view the reality of your experience?"[30] Over 95 percent of the respondents replied that their experience was *definitely real,* 4 percent responded that their experience was *probably real* and the remaining *0.4 percent* thought it *was probably, or definitely, not real.* The overwhelming majority believed their experience was real. The study participants included professionals such as scientists, nurses, physicians, and lawyers. The article's conclusion (in part) is that, "The combination of the preceding nine lines of evidence converges on the conclusion that near-death experiences are medically inexplicable."[31] For Dr. Long, the evidence suggests that "... NDEs are, in a word, real."[32]

A number of authors have written books to share their NDEs. If you are curious, you can find some fascinating reads on your favorite book sellers' website. The one I have chosen to share with you, by Anita Moorjani (in Step One below), is the best example (that I know of), and describes an NDE in extremely vivid detail. Anita's NDE resulted in (what some may consider to be) a miraculous healing of a certain-death terminal illness.

In the final chapter of this book, I compare descriptions of Anita's experience against the backdrop of (what I consider to be) *facts* described in the manuscript I share in Chapter 7. Therefore, without further ado, I present to you, Step One.

Finally ... Step One.
This section of the book introduces you to a new concept of yourself and provides you with a descriptive glimpse of your future.

Step One: Stretching Your Consciousness.

Required Reading: *Dying to be Me* by Anita Moorjani[33]
This astounding book is Anita Moorjani's first published work. *Dying to be Me* is her story of a personal, enlightening NDE experience that changed her life. About Anita, Wikipedia says:

> "Currently, she resides in California.... She was born to Indian parents and when she was very young, the family moved to Hong Kong. Consequently, Anita is multilingual...she speaks English, Cantonese, and an Indian dialect interchangeably."[34]

Anita Moorjani was diagnosed with cancer in April 2002. For four years, she battled the advancing cancer as it slowly progressed. Then the cancer became more aggressive, and one month before she turned forty-seven, Anita fell into a coma and was taken to the hospital. When admitted to the hospital, her body was wasting away, riddled with large malignant tumors. She had open skin lesions that were weeping with toxins. She had a buildup of fluid in her lungs, extreme difficulty breathing, and she needed oxygen to breathe. The admitting doctors were shocked at her condition and told her family she would not last the night.

After twenty-four hours in a coma, Anita woke up, sat up, and declared to her family that she would be okay. She recovered fully within days. After two weeks, the medical team could not find a trace of cancer in her body. After five weeks in hospital and much protesting about ongoing tests trying to find the cancer, the medical team finally conceded and released her from hospital.

During her coma, Anita had had an NDE, which she describes in vivid detail in her book. It is a truly remarkable account of what happens after the death of the body.

Why is this book important to read? Anita expresses clearly (and describes in colorful language) what she thought and felt during her coma. In addition, she brought back many hopeful and inspiring messages. Although one may not fully grasp the true meaning of her words, she provides information and a vivid description of a new impression of self that increases our insights and perceptions of life after death. These understandings will help you stretch your concepts of self and open your mind. The picture she paints will help you grasp the truths presented to you in the remaining chapters of this book.

Anita's transformational experience can be likened to someone who does not know how to paint waking up one morning and painting like Leonardo da Vinci.

Anita experienced our *end-state* but was not given the knowledge of how we can attain this nirvana while in the materialized human state. As such, she has a profound and everlasting concept/experience of where we come from and return to but cannot provide an explanation of the process of creation or how to attain our true purpose in life.

I believe we can all achieve the same awareness and feelings that Anita writes about without having an NDE. In this book, I share a step-by-step process that can lead us to this same remarkable, profound experience. This is the process I followed and present to you in the following chapters. It is an incremental, gradual process that I believe can reward you with the same insights and perceptions Anita experienced.

I can make this last statement because that is what I experienced (and continue to experience) after following the process laid out in this book—that is, following the *Seven Steps*, beginning with the required reading outlined above in this chapter.

I want you to experience what I have experienced—and continue to experience: peace, tranquility, joy, and unconditional love. Be patient, do the work, and know that with time, benefits that are almost impossible to imagine can be yours.

But you must do the work.

PART IV

THE TRUTHS UNVEILED

Look deep into nature,
and then you will understand everything better.[35]
—Albert Einstein

NOTE TO READER...

When your ego is in control, your coffers overflow, and your life is filled with pleasure and ease. You are not compelled to seek Truth; you seek only methods by which to fill human greed.

*There is no difference between you who have little in life and those who have it all, for rich and poor alike get sick, make enemies, find themselves alone. But the potential for you gaining more than the religious and rich can ever hope to gain, in health, happiness, good fellowship, achievement in your chosen way of life, is enormous. And when it is all accomplished, you will **know that the opportunities, the ability, the inspiration** all came from the [Divine] **within**, because you will **know** you could never have done such things if you had not asked the [Divine] within you to help you use all your talents, to put plenty of food in your cupboards, and clothes on your back and happiness and a good life for your children.*

*All these things will the [Divine] **do** for you, if you will but ask – and believe – and know – and remember at all times – that it is the '[Divine] **Nature**' to create and then provide abundantly for all **Its** creation.*[36]

When a person experiences illness, depression, pain, and misery, are they not impelled to seek answers about life and existence in order to find their way out of these undesirable states? It is this seeking, this questioning, that opens people up to first seek and then be receptive to new knowledge and new possibilities. This is what happened to me, and for that I am grateful.

Over my first fifty-seven years, my creative tools provided me with *timely lessons* and moved me toward my *real path*. The pain and misery I experienced drove me to ask questions about life— and about existence itself. Eventually, *I found the path to true spiritual perception and experience;* and it brought me peace, joy, and abundance. I am eternally grateful for the pain and misery I suffered at my own hand and sincerely remorseful for the pain and suffering I caused others. Over the following pages, I share with you secrets hidden since the beginning of creation. The blueprint manuscript shared below and the secrets it contains are "the seeds of the future spiritual evolution of humankind."[37] If you accept them; plant them in your consciousness; and then tend them, nurture them, and bring them into the light, you too will be blessed with a harvest of love, peace, joy, and abundance in your every experience.

—D. Neil Elliott

Chapter 7

MIND AND MATTER: THE FOUNDATION OF SPIRITUAL ENLIGHTENMENT

If you correct your mind,
the rest of your life will fall into place.[38]
—Lao-tzu

Previously I described the type of thoughts and emotions I felt in the wee hours of the night, after a dream or nightmare or while lying awake, rehashing all of my woes. Needless to say, these thoughts affected me throughout the day as well and expressed themselves in moodiness, sharp words of disdain, judgment or condemnation, or careless actions that affected others. Internally, I believed I was a thoughtful, loving person who just had a lot of crap in my life created by external events entirely out of my control. Sometimes, I believed I was just "dealt a bad hand" and that I needed to deal with it. Through these hardships (or so I believed) I would grow stronger. As Nietzsche famously said: "That which does not kill us makes us stronger."[39]

Life is full of ups and downs. Through hard work, smarts, determination, and luck, sometimes wonderful, joyous, and fun things happened for me—but often, no matter how hard I tried, they did not. Through sheer bad luck or being thwarted by others, or because of external circumstances, things did not materialize the way I had hoped. This is life. People (myself included) reminded me to "grow up" and "quit feeling sorry for myself," suggesting I be thankful for all the things I already had. I was reminded that, "Neil, you're smart, educated, you have good friends, a nice house, you make a lot of money." Apparently, I had nothing to complain about. All true. But as life wore on, this is not how I felt.

As I said earlier, I was sick and tired of being sick and tired. My dreams were dashed—and I ended up at that kitchen table crafting that suicide note. It was at this point that I came across the information I am going to share with you. I was at the end of my rope—anything that offered hope was worth exploring.

The title of the blueprint document that changed my life, a set of nine "Letters," might arouse in you preconceived notions as to what it is about and what you can learn from it. I urge you to suspend judgment. Come to this information with an open mind, a seeking mind—like a child, be curious, non-judgmental, and fearless. Hopefully, the books I recommended earlier will have helped you to open your mind so you can take in radical new ideas about the reality of our world and being human. What you are about to read will take you even further into that place that science alone can never penetrate—the Truth of Being, the Truth of our Spiritual Origins, and the Truth of Life and Existence.

Recorded in the "Letters" is the simple *Truth of Our Origins* and *Our Reality of Being*; why and how we create our experiences in life; and how we can Master our creative tools, control the ego, and ascend spiritually. This *reality* remains constant. If you practice the teachings as described and if you act on the new knowledge you gain, you can change the course of your life and set yourself free from the bondage of the ego. Once you are free from the bondage of the ego, you too can experience rapturous joy, absolute peace, and perfect contentment. This process, (applying these lessons) will remove your burdens, despair, and grief. I followed this process to find my way out of ignorance, rid myself of all things inimical to my health, and move into wellbeing, peace, joy, and abundance. If you read the "Letters," understand them, and follow the teachings, you too can utilize this process to "...help your soul emerge from the confines of your ego drive and embark on a new programme of 'thought-emotional-living'..."[40]/[41] that will be more rewarding than you ever dreamed possible.

These teachings are only given at this juncture in human history—at the start of this new millennium—because scientific discovery and understanding have evolved enough that we have the ability to understand, in a logical and realistic way, their concepts and principles. For those who can understand them, they will *bridge the gulf between science and spirituality*. The "Letters" have multiple purposes:

- "...[They are] **exclusively** directed at assisting you to open your consciousness to newness of life, vitality and spiritual power that you may abandon your old way of limited and dis-satisfied living and find a new source of inner joy and fulfilment of your every need."[42]

- "...[Their intent is] to show you the TRUE NATURE of ... 'THAT' ... WHICH BROUGHT YOU INTO BEING – gave you INDIVIDUALITY. For, without this knowledge, which will reveal to you the 'nature' of your 'dual, yet fully inter-related being', Spirit and body, you will also remain rooted in the same level of consciousness as you are at this moment."[43]

And

- "...[Their intent is] expressly to help science bridge the gulf between UNIVERSAL CONSCIOUSNESS and the appearance of electrical particles. Without this bridge between the Unseen Spiritual Dimension and the Seen world of 'matter', science will remain rooted in old ideas and concepts instead of moving forward into new realms of spiritual/scientific research for the betterment of mankind."[44]

In order to fulfill these purposes, you will be introduced to a new "terminology designed to stretch your minds to embrace what 'really is' beyond all earthly form, color, sound, emotion, and comprehension."[45] After reading the manuscript, you will be able to understand the important differences "...between UNIVERSAL CONSCIOUSNESS, Divine Consciousness, and human consciousness. You truly need to understand these differences to enable you to live spiritually pro-active lives within your world...."[46] The "Letters" provide the teachings and process to help you achieve just that, to live spiritually pro-active lives.

My dearest wish is that you will join me in helping to change the consciousness of the world by following the *Seven Steps* offered in this book and spiritualizing your mental processes. Together, let's change our world's collective consciousness from negativity, hate, racism, selfishness, and greed to love, peace, joy, abundance, and acceptance of all. Please help me and other souls to change this planet's collective consciousness by changing yourself first. This blueprint manuscript transformed my life. I hope it can help you transform yours. But before I present this manuscript to you, I will give you the background of how it came to be and how it was shared with the world.

Please know that if you go the Recorder's website (listed later in this chapter), or to other related websites, typically they portray significant overtones of conventional Christianity. If the religious images or language used on these sites invokes within you displeasing connotations, please ignore the websites and subdue the negative feelings. Such "branding" of this material almost made me flee from learning the teachings. But remember, I was agnostic and at the end of my rope. I was seeking anything that would relieve my pain and misery. So I ignored the religious depictions and rhetoric and forged on. I am so glad I did!

In or around March 1919, a baby girl was born. She grew up to be a devout Christian. When she was about forty years old and experiencing severe difficulties, she prayed for help. During her time in prayer, a sudden and powerful answer came through to her that caused her to re-examine her beliefs and discard all religious dogma. Enlightenment followed.

Over the next forty years, she was taken through various personal circumstances: successes, joy, failures, pain, and misery. During this time, she was guided. She learned valuable life lessons and transcended them spiritually. Her consciousness was cleansed slowly. In or about the year 2000 A.D. (the Recorder was eighty-one), Christ communicated with her clearly and dictated the material (the nine "Letters") you will soon be more formally introduced to.[47]

You will learn from Christ that this woman was chosen especially for this work prior to her birth. She was told to keep her name off the material and to remain anonymous; just as a secretary that takes dictation on a business letter remains anonymous.

Christ explains in the "Letters" that his only means of reaching us has been through a human being who is sensitive and clairaudient; born to be a channel through whom he could review our current human condition. He explains that "[He has] been able to intimately review the conflict and pain unknown in centuries past because scientific and technological discoveries, and the lessening of moral and conventional values, have led to new highly stressful conditions of modern living and new ways of relating to each other."[48] Through the mind of the woman who calls herself simply "the Recorder," our modern human condition became, to a slight degree, subjective for him. He explains further that "Without this knowledge of the human experience, these Letters could not have been written in a form which is intended to be helpful to the human condition at this time."[49] As such, Christ is aware of all that has happened during the last two millennia, since his death on the cross, and explains that "THESE LETTERS are a MASTER'S COURSE,"[50] leveraging our current scientific understandings to teach us "...the spiritual-scientific REALITY from which [we] have derived [our] being."[51] The "Letters'" Foreword, Introduction, and part of "Letter 1" explain more fully the circumstances and purpose behind the "Letters."

Overview of the "Letters" – What You Will Learn

The "Letters" tell a story, just as this book and other non-fiction books and novels tell a story. "Letter 1" opens with an introduction that explains why and how the "Letters" came about. Christ explains why he has returned at this *crucial time in our history* and why he has used a human being to record his words. He reveals the purpose behind the "Letters" and shares significant spiritual facts (such as that there is no such thing as a "sin against a God," and that we do not understand the Truth of Our Being). He tells us that "... [we] are on the threshold of a world crisis of enormous proportions, [and that] it is vital for survival that I, the Christ, should reach all who will listen."[52] He clarifies that, "You know little of the true processes of creation in which you ... play a major role."[53] He tells us that as individuals, we bring forth our own pain and misery, and that collectively, humankind brings forth its own collective pain, misery, and wars. He informs us that, "It is imperative you ... understand them [your creative tools] ... to enable you to ... [implement] a higher vision for all humanity"[54] and he explains that not only were his teachings during his time on Earth misunderstood but since the time those misunderstandings were recorded in the New Testament, they have misled people. He discloses what his true mission on Earth was and describes his life prior to being baptized in the River Jordan, and then continues his personal story, sharing a vivid description of what really happened to him during his six-week sojourn in the desert; what he was shown, what he learned, and the knowledge that changed him from rebel to teacher and healer.

In this fascinating read, Christ shares the strident temptations that occurred to him at the end of his desert experience and realizes that they were not *temptations by the devil*. Instead, they were a tug-of-war between the humanly entrenched ego drive and the Father-Mother Consciousness that had made itself known to him.

In "Letter 2," Christ shares more details of his life story: What happened when he returned to Nazareth, the events that led up to his first public healing, the start of his three-year mission, and how he chose his disciples. He continues with stories of his public teachings and what he actually told the people. These stories are enlightening, to say the least. If you read and ponder them, you can gain an understanding of why his teachings were not understood by the people of his day. The stories he relays are clear as you read them; however, as you spend the time and make the effort to complete the work as outlined in the seven-step process offered to you in this book, they will become *crystal clear*.

In "Letter 3," Christ continues the story of his teachings and describes vividly more events and life experiences. He realizes that his time on Earth will be cut short through crucifixion and chronicles what really happened before and at the Last Supper, his disciples' responses and attitudes, and he describes clearly the truth regarding his ascension. The stories relayed are spiritually enlightening. Again, *you must comprehend* his account of the life he led before and after his desert experience and what was really revealed to him in the desert to understand the reason his teachings were so grossly misinterpreted. Your realization of this truth is vital so that you may know that the teachings in these "Letters" could only come from one source, that source being the one who experienced that life, the man known as Jesus.

The knowledge shared in "Letters 1 to 3" are foundational for your understanding of the future knowledge and the true processes of creation that will be shared with you in later "Letters." In "Letter 4," Christ gathers up the threads of his teachings in Palestine and speaks about the Buddha, Muhammad, and all other Masters that have continued to develop spiritually and have ascended in consciousness. He explains that although they each have retained their individuality; they are all equal. He explains further the truth regarding sexual relationships— how men's and women's attitudes regarding sexuality will change eventually, that spiritual progress will take place, and how that evolution will facilitate the birth of children with new spiritual potential. In this "Letter," Christ uses the image of rain as an analogy to describe your soul. He describes the unity of all souls—regardless of one's religion or race, color or beliefs, attitudes or upbringing, wealth or poverty, social status or birthplace, or circumstances in life.

You will remember from Step One that Anita Moorjani also recorded from her experience that "Everything belongs to an infinite Whole. I was intricately, inseparably enmeshed with all of life. We're all facets of that unity—we're all One, and each of us has an effect on the collective Whole."[55]

"Letter 5" and "Letter 6" begin the teachings on the process of creation. Christ explains what both science and religious doctrines believe—and he rejects those beliefs. He clarifies why science has evolved as it has and how and why it will remain locked behind the closed doors of a wholehearted belief in materialism (that it has established for itself and by which it explains creation) until some enlightened scientists defy convention and investigate the realm of mind and spirit properly. He utilizes an extremely helpful in-depth story regarding current scientific knowledge that will assist us readers to grow in awareness, preparing us for the explanation of the *Truth of Being*. He introduces the truth regarding the human ego—a necessary tool of creation and the means of earthly individuality but also the source of all misery, suffering, and despair. These "Letters" explain *Our Truth*, the *Truth of Existence*, and the *Truth of Creation*.

I urge you to read "Letter 1" through "Letter 4" in their entireties, even though you may be tempted to skip them to get onto what you consider to be the *Heart of the Matter*, the Truth of Existence and the Truth of Creation. If you jump past these letters and move on to read "Letter 5" and "Letter 6" first, you will have missed out on the slow, deliberate building of your foundational learning and new knowledge. I highly recommend that you *do not do this*! This new knowledge is designed to open your mind further to the Truth. To get the most out of these teachings—and to gain knowledge that will enable you to transform your life properly—start at "Letter 1" and read each "Letter" in sequence.

In "Letter 7," Christ explains "the truth concerning the sexual act; the truth of what takes place both spiritually and physically. In addition, he reveals how and why children are born on different levels of consciousness, and discloses the reality of men's and women's place in the world order."[56]

In "Letter 8," the reality of men and women is expanded upon. Christ describes clearly how to live within the LAWS of EXISTENCE, how to come into a new state of being, and how you can transform your current reality into one of a harmonious blessed state. It is a state "…in which all things are abundantly provided, health is restored, and joy becomes a natural state of mind. Every individual can reach this interior state of blessedness, and peace will then become the norm."[57] This state, Christ tells us, can be ours.

In "Letter 9," "Christ ties up the loose ends of his other Letters and tells people plainly how to overcome the ego, gain true self-esteem, and experience the joy of perfect inner peace. He touches on racism and gives a personal message of encouragement and love to all who are drawn to his Letters."[58] In this "Letter," he also uses a marvelous, colorful analogy when explaining the purpose of reincarnation. He clarifies that "... [reincarnation] is not haphazard or without a consistent plan directing its action."[59]

Step Two: Truths Unveiled.

Required Reading: Christ Returns – Speaks His Truth (the "Letters"):
Daily Reading, Pondering, and Reflecting on the "Letters."
(Referenced as the "Letters" and in Notes as "Christ's Letters." Links are provided at the end of this chapter for your complimentary .pdf and/or audio file download.)

The "Letters," as previously mentioned, were dictated energetically by Christ and were captured by a woman in 2000 A.D. She says that Christ told her clearly to: *"...leave myself out of the picture [and] that Christ's Letters must stand entirely on their own. People must decide for themselves whether the Letters rang true or whether people felt they were fake."* [60]

At this point in the reading, I suggest that if you are holding any disbelieving thoughts or judgments, that you hold these lightly. If you doubt the veracity of this story, don't give those thoughts credence, for such thinking will create barriers which may prevent you from experiencing a change of heart and thought as you continue reading the "Letters." The Recorder explains that: *"What is truly important is whether the reader can feel this is the authentic Christ who has risen in spiritual consciousness to the very portals of the Equilibrium whilst still retaining individuality in order to remain in contact with the world of individuality."* [61]

"Letter 1" through "Letter 9" contain fundamental learnings, key to building your foundation and solidifying the new knowledge that will enable you to transform your life. After the Recorder channeled the "Letters" in the year 2000/2001, Christ dictated an additional sixteen Articles and three Messages (in 2007, 2010, and 2014) to the Recorder. In reference to these Articles, Christ says: "I have come this time, not to speak beautiful passages of spiritual encouragement to arouse your spiritual yearnings but to reach into your daily lives with your own colloquial language to shed LIGHT on what people are daily doing to themselves – their bodies, lives, relationships and to the planet generally."[62]

These Articles complement the learnings in the "Letters" and, indeed, reference the "Letters" directly. The *nine "Letters" will be your focus* for a year or more until you have fully grasped the Truth of your Existence. However, read the Articles too because they contribute additional examples, in colloquial language, to reinforce the learnings in the "Letters." Anyone who has not spent the necessary time in meditation, prayer, and in studying the "Letters" (in order to cleanse their consciousness properly and be fully receptive of these spiritual truths) will not completely understand the three Messages (from 2007, 2010, and 2014). They are worth reading (and I recommend you read them), but please know: Comprehending their true spiritual meaning may escape you until you have absorbed and understood the teachings shared in the "Letters."

The 2010 Message is a direct appeal to adherents of the Christian faith to let go of their religious doctrines and dogma and wake up to the Truth of Existence as explained in the "Letters." The 2007 and 2014 Messages were dictated to further assist those who have—and continue to—study the "Letters." The purpose of the 2007 Message is to bring a greater clarity to your understanding of the "Letters" and provide clear instructions to help you "…become the loving creative individual who is needed to bring about the Era of Peace so passionately longed for by people on earth and yet so passionately withstood [resisted] by people on earth."[63] The 2014 Message explains how to achieve this Higher Vision and bring it into being, which outcome all humanity should strive to attain, for it will bring all of humanity into a *New Era of Love and Peace.* But it takes time for individuals to adopt and implement new learnings in order to absorb and achieve new growth and enlightenment. This enlightenment is achieved through the gradual spiritualization of your mental processes and cleansing of your consciousness outlined in the *Steps* I am sharing with you.

I can understand why some readers may question the veracity of these "Letters." You may have preconceived notions as to what you will be learning. As to the verification of their truthfulness, that is up to you. However, I can tell you that what you will read about and learn *is probably not what you are expecting.* In addition—and this bears repeating again—I can testify that if you do the readings, learn the new knowledge, and follow the *Seven Steps* outlined in this book, *you can transform your life.* Peace, rapturous joy, tranquility, abundance, and prosperity can be yours if you can put your current beliefs aside, put your mind to learning the spiritual Truth of your origins, and take the necessary steps to ascend spiritually.

Tips for Doing this Work

1. With reference to the "Letters," suspend your desire to discuss with anyone what you are reading or why you are

reading it. This includes your spouse, your kids, everyone. Do not disclose the title of the material or what you are learning. Why am I suggesting this? Sharing what you are reading and learning will create conversations with others. Their responses and reactions, if negative or doubtful, may undermine your learning and your progress, which may, in turn, create doubts in your mind. Doubts create barriers; blockages that will prevent you from learning and accepting the spiritual truths on offer. Sharing will come later, when your understanding is both deep and unshakeable.

2. Read the "Letters" in order: Foreword, Introduction, and so on. Be patient, and do not skip ahead. Please note that the "Letters" can be challenging to *read* because of the unusual formatting. I suggest you read them a page at a time or download the free audio files and listen to them while relaxing in your favorite chair. By listening to an audio file, you can enjoy the *story and teachings* without being distracted by the unusual formatting. In addition, the tips for listening to an audio file, offered in Chapter Six of this book, may improve your concentration and focus. That will be of great benefit when you are learning the meditation technique recommended in the "Letters."

3. Do all the exercises when asked to do so, including the cupping of the hands when explaining the reality of the soul and the ego and the placing of the palms together when explaining the meaning of what is meant by equilibrium.

4. Create a comfortable, private meditation spot where you will not be disturbed. I use a recliner in our spare room. I have asked that no one disturb me when I'm meditating. I use soft foam earplugs to block out noises and distractions. This is also my extended reading and listening space.

5. I suggest strongly that you disconnect from all media and entertainment that use emotive language or portray any

other "mental food" contrary to LOVE. If you believe your food intake is important (and it is), your mental diet is even more important. Keep it clean and nutritious.

6. All of this will take time. So, be patient, be kind, be loving to yourself. As noted, DO NOT DOUBT, as this will set you back immeasurably.

7. Keep an open mind and do not prejudge.

8. Unlike reading an entertaining novel, these "Letters" are meant to be PONDERED. It is not a race. You are here to understand and learn. So, be thoughtful. Take the time to contemplate the meaning of each passage as you read (or listen).

Step Three: Reflection.

Required Exercise: Write Yourself a Letter.

When you are asked to write yourself a letter, follow the instructions and do it. Date it, seal it, and open it a year later. DO NOT SKIP this step! Keep it safe. Keep it private. This letter is for YOU and ONLY you. Be brutally honest when writing it—it is for your eyes only.

Now on to the required readings for Step Two and letter writing in Step Three.

A link to both a complimentary .pdf version of Christ's *"Letters"* and a related audio files can be found at DNeilElliott. com/Resources.

In the next chapter I share four excerpts (and a fifth in a later chapter) from the "Letters" to give you a taste, a sample of the writing, and a glimpse of the sheer brilliance of the author, Christ, in explaining complex concepts in simple, everyday language.

Chapter 8

A PEEK INSIDE

People only see what they are prepared to see.[64]
—Ralph Waldo Emerson

The best way to introduce you to the "Letters" is to give you a taste of the writing through the following four excerpts from this densely rich three-hundred-plus-page treasure trove of Truths. But first, an important note: The "Letters" use unusual formatting to emphasize specific words and phrases. The italics, bold print, capitals, underlining, and the hard returns in the middle of sentences may interfere with your natural flow of reading. But, as the Recorder says, "...this is just the point. [The "Letters" are] not meant to be read. [They are] meant to be PONDERED and this means you have to stop on the words in print which hold up the flow of words and THINK about what the words are trying to convey to you."[65]

That said, for your ease of reading, I have changed the complex formatting of all the excerpts (noted as "Excerpts") in this book to italics and retained some of the uppercase format and bolding as is. Note also that the spelling is British, and in order to quote the Recorder's manuscript verbatim, the syntax, spelling, punctuation, and grammatical errors that were in the original have been retained. Also, throughout the "Letters," and especially when relaying the story of his life on Earth, two thousand years ago, in the persona of Jesus (in "Letters 1 through 3"), Christ refers to the "Father" when referring to the Source of our Being. In the "Letters" Christ explains that:

"When I was on earth, I made a distinction between 'Your Father in Heaven' and 'Your Father within you'. When I spoke of 'Your FATHER in heaven', I meant UNIVERSAL INTELLIGENCE."[66]

Due to the Jewish practice of subordinating women in the ancient world, Jesus coined the term the "Father" to avoid Jewish resistance to his teachings and to gain acceptance of the new terminology. He says:

Because of the Jewish attitude to women, I only referred to this aspect of UNIVERSAL CONSCIOUSNESS. Now, to you who are so aware of the equality of genders, I speak of: 'FATHER-MOTHER-CONSCIOUSNESS' in equilibrium within UNIVERSAL CONSCIOUSNESS/AWARENESS where 'Father Consciousness – is – Universal Intelligence' [and] 'Mother Consciousness – is – Universal Love'.[67]

So, in the excerpts below, you will see references to the "Father." (One further note: The terms and spiritual components of consciousness mentioned in the quote above are fully explained in later "Letters.")

Forewarned is forearmed, as the saying goes. If you would like to read the original .pdf manuscript, it is available as a download at DNeilElliott.com/Resources.

So, on to Excerpt One.

Excerpt One:

Human Consciousness Must be Speedily Uplifted

*Therefore, to save you from your own folly expressed through the media and TV, the 'human consciousness' must be SPEEDILY uplifted to see **what I saw in the desert** – the **Reality of Love** behind and within all existence.*

*N.B. When this great truth is both perceived and warmly acknowledged, the **Reality of Love** will begin to manifest Itself in multiple ways in every living thing and in the environment itself.*

*The experience of abundance and joy will re-enforce the consciousness of abundance and joy. **And so, a spiritual spiral of ever more exalted and wondrous living will be set in motion.***

When the TRUE nature of 'Being' is fully understood – humanity will move on to the next rung of spiritual evolution and will put into motion a new and blessed form of human endeavor and personal experience. To achieve these goals, humanity must first gain insight into:

WHAT and WHO you are.

*A new and important question is already coming into people's consciousness. 'Who are you – really – behind the facade you present to the world?' What does it take to be **REAL?***

It is this question of 'Who you really are' which is answered, on every level of your being, within these pages. **And if you can accept as your own guidelines for daily living – all that I understood during my six-weeks 'desert' experience – you too will eventually become WHOLE and REAL even as I became WHOLE and REAL before I commenced my ministry of healing and teaching.**[68]

Excerpt Two:

Can You See What I Saw?

MY BAPTISM

When I entered the water in the River Jordan to be baptized by John, I expected to feel nothing more than relief that I had, for once, taken a positive step in reforming my behavior. I expected to feel a new determination to go home and astonish my mother and neighbors with my new kindly attitudes towards them.

What really happened when John baptized me was an experience completely different to anything I had ever thought possible.

I felt a great wave of tremendous energy surge through my body. I was literally stunned by it. As I staggered out of the river, I felt myself elevated in consciousness in a most extraordinary way. A great inflow of glowing happiness uplifted me to a state of ecstasy. I was enraptured and aware of a great Light.

Stumbling, I moved away from the river and walked and walked, not knowing where I was going. I continued on, unseeingly, into the desert.

Please note! MY SIX WEEKS IN THE DESERT were a time of total inner cleansing of my human consciousness. Old attitudes, beliefs and prejudices were dissolved.

The time has come for me to share with receptive people all that I felt, 'saw', realised and understood.

(To help people abandon the age-old imaginative pictures of a biblical 'deity' I will avoid referring to 'God' by that word and will use a terminology designed to stretch your minds to embrace what 'really is' beyond all earthly form, color, sound, emotion, and comprehension. This terminology will become ever more meaningful as you persevere in meditation and prayer.)

WHAT I FELT WHEN IN THE DESERT
I was uplifted into inner radiant light and felt vibrant and wondrously alive with power. I was filled with ecstasy and joy and I knew beyond all doubt that THIS POWER was the true Creator out of which all created things had been given their being.

This glorious interior harmony, peace, and sense of perfect fulfillment, needing nothing more to be added to that beautiful moment, was the very nature of the Reality – the Creative Power – giving Life to creation and existence.

What I 'saw', realized, perceived when in the desert.
I was lifted into another dimension of conscious perception, which enabled me to see the TRUTH concerning life and existence. I saw, lucidly and clearly, what was real and what was false in man's thinking.

I realized that this 'Creative Power' I was experiencing was infinite, eternal, universal, filling all space beyond

123

sky, oceans, earth, and all living things. I saw IT was MIND POWER.

IT was the CREATIVE POWER of MIND.

There was no point where this 'DIVINE CREATIVE POWER OF MIND' was not. I realized that human mind was drawn from DIVINE CREATIVE MIND but was only a candle lit by the sun.

At times, my human sight was so spiritually heightened, I could see through rocks, earth, sand. These now appeared to be only a 'shimmer of tiny 'motes'.

I realized that nothing was really solid!

When I had moments of doubt that this could be so, the changes in the phenomena stopped taking place, and much later, I discovered that: my thoughts, if strongly imbued with CONVICTION could effect changes in the 'shimmer of motes' (what science presently calls electrically charged particles) and therefore produce changes in the appearance of the rock or whatever I was studying.

It was at this point, that I came to realize the powerful effect that CONVICTION or unwavering FAITH had on the environment when stating a command or even a belief.

What was even more startling was my mind-opening, 'cosmic consciousness' realisation that all I had been witnessing was really the **'Creative Power'** *of* **Divine Mind** *Itself made visible in the 'shimmer of tiny motes'.*

Not only this, its **appearance** *could be profoundly affected by the activity of human thought.*

I realized there was nothing solid in the universe, everything visible was manifesting a differing 'state of consciousness' which determined the composition and form of the 'shimmer of motes'. **Therefore, all outer form was an expression of the inner consciousness.**

LIFE and CONSCIOUSNESS, I realized, were one and the same thing.

It was impossible to say 'This is LIFE' and 'That is CONSCIOUSNESS'.

Consciousness was Life, and Life was Consciousness and was the **'Creative Power'** *of both;* **DIVINE UNIVERSAL MIND'** *beyond, within and behind the universe.*

I realized that people placed highest importance on **individuality and form.** *They could not imagine mind or intelligence operating in any effective way other than through the medium of individual form. Because of this, the Jews had created a mental image of a vast supreme being, having all the attributes, positive and negative, of a human being. Thus was it possible for prophets to believe in – and speak of – Jehovah's anger, threats of punishment, visitations of sickness and plagues in response to human waywardness. But these mental images, I realized were myths. They did not exist.*

I perceived that, in any dimension of existence, it was the MIND – the intelligence exhibited – which was the all-important factor relating to creation and man, himself. Therefore, Genesis should be rewritten: Before creation – was **UNIVERSAL MIND – Creative Power behind and within creation itself.**

Having 'seen' so clearly, beyond all dispute, that the Creative Power of UNIVERSAL MIND was everywhere, within the infinity of the skies and active within earthly forms as well, I was inwardly directed to look around me and saw only gravel and rock. Then, suddenly I was presented with a picture of a beautiful land in which were growing every conceivable plant, shrub and tree, even birds flitted in the trees, and animals grazed the grass.

Watching this vision with amazement, I 'saw' that plants and trees, every one of them – and yes, even birds and animals, in reality, were composed of hundreds of communities of infinitely tiny entities (your modern scientists call them 'cells') working continuously, in an entirely harmonious spirit of cooperation, to produce the substance and various organs of the inner system and the outer appearance of the completed living entity.

I contemplated this wonderful activity for a long time, although time was no longer of any importance to me. As I gazed and gazed, I thought, **'Who would have guessed that within the outer covering of fur, feather, skin, there was such intense activity within tiny communities of entities, working together to give life, form, nutrition, healing, protection, endurance to the bodies of so many different species.'**

It was the intelligently performed WORK which attracted my attention.

Therefore, **WORK,** *I realized was an integral part of the* **Creative Power Activity** *from the very least 'entity' (cell) within living systems to the most advanced entity in the universe – man himself. In the systems of all living things, all the labor was under the direction, ultimately, of the* **Divine Creative Power,** *in whom were the plans and designs of creation. I saw that these plans and designs were, in reality,*

126

'consciousness forms' and could be termed WORDS, since each WORD signifies a very special 'consciousness' form.

Hence the original WORD in **'Creative Power Consciousness'** becomes manifested in the visible world. The WORD, and therefore the **'Consciousness Pattern'** remains within the **DIVINE CREATIVE MIND** continually bringing forth its own.

I could 'see' then, that everything in the universe, did 'live, move and have its being' in the **Creative Power** of **UNIVERSAL MIND** which was infinite and eternal and was the only true **Reality** behind all manifestations of individualized form.

I was filled with praise that everything in the world was out of, and yet within this superlative **Creative Power of Divine Mind**. I marveled at all this secret activity forever taking place in all living things, including human bodies, and wondered how it was that such infinitely small units worked intelligently according to specified plans to produce, unerringly, the proposed form – tree trunk, leaf, flower, fruit, insects, birds, animals and human bodies.

I then realized, even more clearly, that the **'Creative Power'** was the very **Source** of **all 'intelligent activity' in the universe.**

If mankind possessed intelligence, it was only because he had drawn it from the **'Universal Source of All Being'**.

Furthermore, I was shown that the **Divine Creative Power** always worked according to certain fundamental and exact principles of construction.

I was shown that:

Just as men have clear characteristics and a well-defined 'nature' in their self-presentation to the world at large, so did the CREATIVE POWER possess a clearly defined 'Nature' – distinct characteristics – which could be clearly recognized in the manner that all living things, plants, animals, birds, men, were constructed and maintained.

I 'saw' that these 'principles' and 'characteristics', clearly observable in the process of creation, were set, invariable LAWS governing all of existence.

*These LAWS are so much part of life that they are never questioned. They are undeviating and consistent – but there would be no such laws if there were no **Creative Intelligent Power** manifesting Itself through the universe.*

These 'principles' of creation, the characteristics of the Creative Power Itself, are as follows:
(I am translating them into your present tense because these 'principles' are eternal.)

1. ***The 'Nature' of the 'Creative Power' is GROWTH.***
   *Everything living always grows. **GROWTH** is a universal characteristic, an undeviating principle of existence.*

2. ***The 'Nature' of the 'Creative Power' is NUTRITION and NOURISHMENT.***
   Nutrition and Nourishment are a normal and marvelously organized process within bodies which is evident to all who take the trouble to consider them. Nutrition is provided for all living things according to individual preferences and the food is digested to promote health and well-being. When little creatures are born, milk is already supplied within the mother,

ready and waiting for the newborn. This too is a mystifying principle of existence none can deny.

No science can explain why such a fortuitous function within the system ensuring survival of the species, should have originally come into being. The actual function itself may be understood but not the 'why' and the mainspring of the function.

3. **The 'Nature' of the 'Creative Power' is HEALING.**
Healing is a natural characteristic of existence and can be said to be a natural 'Perfecting Process', which takes place to ensure individual comfort but none can explain what prompts the activity of healing.

4. **The 'Nature' of the 'Creative Power' is PROTECTION.**
Protection is an integral characteristic of Creative Power and all of Its seeming 'miraculous' activity in the world is geared towards protection. (Today, your medical text books describe the various protective systems in your body but when I was in the desert I 'saw' the characteristic of Protection inherent in the Intelligent Creative Power in the following way.)

As plants, birds and animals were presented to me for inspired observation, I could see how every 'need of protection' in bodies has been lovingly supplied, with the greatest attention to detail.

5. **This characteristic of 'Protection' is combined with the other dynamic characteristic of FULFILMENT OF NEED.**
This was made clearly apparent in the provision of hair, fur and feathers to protect the skin of living creatures and to provide warmth in the cold and shelter in the heat. I saw that the tender endings of important and sensitive fingers and

toes were all provided with appropriate protection of hoof and nail. Eyebrows protected eyes from sweat, eyelids and lashes protected eyes from dust and damage. I realized that those animals which attracted flies were equipped with the kind of tails which would most speedily get rid of them.

What a happy, joyous kind of love and caring were expressed in these small physical attributes which seemed so small and inconsequential and yet had such a profound bearing on the comfort of all living things. *These physical luxuries, added to the basic physical design, were clearly the product of an Intelligence which intended creation to be comfortable and happy – free of the stress which would have been experienced by man and beast if these 'luxury items' had not been given them!*

*Even the natural functions were so intelligently and comfortably designed as to call forth thanksgiving. Everything tucked so neatly out of sight. How blest, how fortunate was mankind to be born into a life so wonderfully provided for! Again, my praises soared and I was lifted on an inner golden light of rapturous wonder – for I now 'saw' that, in addition to freedom from stress, living creatures were also meant to express the exuberant loving **NATURE** of the **Creative Power**. For this reason, they were equipped with limbs: arms, hands, legs and feet, fingers and toes, to enable them to move about, run, leap and dance, to be able to express their inmost thoughts and feelings. I even felt that if mankind longed to fly and grow wings and believed with all their hearts they could do so; eventually they would begin growing something additional to enable them to fly.*

*It was at this point of understanding of the **NATURE** of the '**Creative Power**' that I came into the full consciousness of the*

*LOVE directing the **WORKS** of the **Universal Intelligent Creative Power**.*

*As I pondered this **LOVE**, I realized that the 'mother' in creation, nourishes, protects, fulfills the needs and tries to promote healing of offspring; this is the activity of **LOVE**.*

6. ***The innate characteristic of the LOVING INTELLI-GENT CREATIVE POWER which has given creation its individual form and 'being' is WORK.***

It works for us, in us, and through us.

Its 'work' is always, always, always, prompted by LOVE.

*This cosmic revelation filled me with joy and astonishment. What a wonderful world we lived in! It was the culminating point in my enlightenment and my overall view of the **TRUTH** concerning the **SOURCE of ALL BEING**.*

I had already 'seen' the reality of the physical bodies composed of various communities of identical 'infinitely tiny entities' working in a spirit of co-operation and harmony to produce the various components of the body – flesh, bone, blood to eyes and hair.

*The only difference between these communities **lay in the type of work** demanded by their common goals. Surely the **DIVINE IMPULSE** behind all this intelligent, purposeful activity in the body, was both the inspiration and foundation of man's own conduct when people worked in unison to produce a planned objective? They drew intelligence and purpose from the **Creative Power yet how very different was man's behaviour when engaged in earthly construction*** *or any other communal project for it was inevitably characterized by arguments and dissension.*

*I was brought to a realization of the **INFINITE POWER** of the 'Intelligent Creativity' ever active within creation, maintaining order, co-operation, harmony, daily productivity, unequalled by man anywhere, at any time.*

7. **SURVIVAL**
...was a natural characteristic of the 'Creative Power'. In every case, the most wonderful provision had been made for all living things to grow, be healed of illnesses and injury, nourished in order to keep the body healthy, and to produce its own kind in order to ensure survival on this earth. This was the only reality mankind could be absolutely sure of and Its activity was consistent, year in and year out. The sun, moon, stars, all remained in their places for millennia and it was recognized that they all possessed their own paths of movement – this phenomena was all part of the grand scheme for survival in creation.

If this was so, how could there not be survival of the eternal flame of: Loving Intelligent Creative Power hidden within the created entities of every kind in the universe? Therefore, this world was but a shadow and image of the hidden worlds of Loving Intelligent Creative Power beyond this dimension. The Reality of the entirety of creation lay beyond this visible world.

8. **The inherent characteristic of Loving Intelligent Creative Power was RHYTHM. I saw that there was a RHYTHM in operation in the world.**
Everything was subject to seasons which gave a blossoming and burgeoning of life, a growing season coming up to the ripening and harvest, and the production of seeds which ensured the

survival of plant life. Then there was the gradual dying away and rest period of winter. But nothing created and living was allowed to become extinct. The sun and moon expressed these characteristics within the universe. This rhythm could even be seen in the females of living things. Therefore, everything in creation had its due time for appearance and harvest. It followed that man himself was subject to tides of growth and success and tides of dormancy.

9. ***The inherent characteristic of the Loving Intelligent Creative Power was LAW AND ORDER.***

The undeviating order and reliability apparent in creation, even governing the tiny entities ('cells') within the body, were astonishing and far transcended any human endeavor. Therefore, the entire universe was operating under a system of perfect LAW & ORDER.

I realized on ever higher and higher levels of spiritual exaltation that the 'creative power' exhibited intelligent purposefulness and loving concern for all living things. I realized that life was not something nebulous or amorphous but an intelligent loving creative power which I could actually feel within myself as a tremendously heightened state of being, perception, radiance, ecstasy, joy, love. I knew myself to be one with it – filled with it – and I was one with everything around me and one with the sky and stars.

*And – most wonderful and glorious of all – **the very 'Nature' and 'Function' of this 'Father – Creative Power'** was to work in order to create joy, beauty, and comfort to ensure mankind's well-being, to work within mankind to provide interior joy, health and comfort, and to work through mankind, inspiring him with new realization and understanding.*

Wonderful vistas of glorious creativity came to mind. Once we became truly 'at one', purified channels and instruments of the **'Intelligent Creative Power'**, *we could gradually ascend in consciousness until we truly expressed through our minds and hearts the very* **'NATURE'** *of the* **'Universal Creative Power'.** *Then 'life on earth' would indeed become a 'state of heaven' at all times and we would enter into a state of eternal life!*

This must surely be the true goal behind creation, I thought. And it came to me with a surge of elation and loving joy, that this was the purpose for which man had been evolved and developed!

But – even at this present time, although mankind was so very imperfect in his behaviour, absolutely nothing was impossible to him in the future, since, despite his wrongdoing, he was one with the 'Creative Power' and the 'Creative Power' was within him, giving him life, limb, and everything else he needed.

All of this realization lifted me to the heights of rapture, elation and sublime ecstasy, so that I was scarcely able to bear it. I felt my body must dissolve with the expansion of Power within me. I was irradiated with **LIGHT** *and could see* **IT** *all around me illuminating the desert scene.*

My heart sang in praises. How wonderful and beautiful was the Loving Creative Power which worked in, through and for us, unceasingly!

What a MIRACLE was creation!

I cried out loud:
    *'***YOU** *are the* **SOURCE of all BEING***, both creator and also manifested within and through the created: there is*

134

*nothing in the entire universe which is apart or separate from the limitless, eternal infinity of **DIVINE LIFE, Creative Power Consciousness** – that you are – how then is it possible that mankind is so sinful – and why do people suffer disease, misery and poverty? Tell me, o loving **'Father' Creative Power**, because I have been heavily burdened with the pain of their miserable lives.'*

Then I was shown the reality of the 'earthly condition' of all living things.

*I felt immense excitement because, at last, I would be able to understand how it was that such a loving **Divine 'Creative Power'** could allow Its creation to endure such misery.*

I was shown that every living thing in creation should be radiantly healthy, cared for, nourished, protected, healed, maintained in peace and plenty, prospered within an orderly society of 'beings' extending only love to each other.

(However, at the moment of creation, two BASIC IMPULSES came into being, ensuring individuality, and it was these which controlled mankind's consciousness.

These IMPULSES were explained to me in detail but this knowledge is reserved for a future Letter when you will be better able to understand it)....

I was shown the following vivid vision.

First of all, I saw a new-born babe as 'light', a life-form of 'Creative Power'.

As the baby grew into childhood, then manhood, I saw the pure LIGHT of the 'Creative Power' gradually dimmed and then obscured altogether in him, by a dense wrapping of chains and thongs.

I questioned the meaning of the vision and there came to my mind a clear understanding which may be expressed in the following words:

'From birth to death – people believe and insist that their five senses of sight, hearing, touch, smell and taste, correctly predicate the 'reality' of themselves and the universe around them. Therefore, because they draw their mind power direct from Divine 'Creative Power', it is done to them according to their beliefs.

Each thong represents a person's habitual thoughts, responses to people and events, prejudices, hates, animosities, anxieties, sorrows, all of which bind him down and shut out the Light from his inner vision drawn from the 'Creative Power'. Thus, he enters into darkness but does not know it. He believes he is growing up and becoming mature in the ways of the world which will enable him to forge ahead and make 'good' – become successful – the aim of most people on earth.

In fact, the more mature he becomes and versed in worldly ways, the more densely do his chains and thongs imprison him within the grip of the twin IMPULSES of 'Bonding-Rejection'.

Furthermore, each chain is forged out of selfish and deceitful desires, greed, aggression, violence and rape. These chains hang heavy around him and burden the psyche, which is the 'creative consciousness power' deep within him. Chain and thong will bind him tighter with every passing year until he realizes what he is doing to himself and sincerely repents each thong and chain and makes due restitution to others whom he has harmed.

With this vision I learnt a most valuable aspect of existence. Man, himself is born with all the potential to make a beautiful life for himself but he, himself, by indulging his selfish desires and hatreds, creates a prison of misery for himself from which there was no escape until such times as he realizes the **TRUTH OF EXISTENCE.**

All the problems of harsh existence lay within the thought processes of man himself!

Only people's 'consciousness forms', their thoughts, words, feelings, actions created a dense barrier between their consciousness and the Universal Creative Consciousness interpenetrating the universe in every leaf, tree, insect, bird, animal and human being.

I was also shown the LAWS OF EXISTENCE controlling the human ability to create new circumstances and environment, relationships, achievement or failure, prosperity or poverty.

Whatever man profoundly **BELIEVES** *himself to be, good or bad, that will he become.*

Whatever man **FEARS** *others will do to him, so will they do.*

Whatever man **HOPES** *that others will do to him, he must first do to them, since he is then creating a 'consciousness pattern' which will return to bless him to the extent he has blest others.*

*Whatever disease man **DREADS** so will he become prey to it for he will have created a 'consciousness pattern' of the very thing he least wants to experience.*

Whatever is sent forth from man's mind and heart – returns to him in due course in some form or another, but remember that like always breeds like. Strongly emotional thoughts are 'consciousness seeds' planted within a man's own orbit of consciousness. These will grow, bearing a like harvest for his reaping.

These are the fruits of free will.

There is no way that man may escape what he thinks, says or does – for he is born of the Divine Creative Consciousness power and is likewise creative in his imagining.

Those who long for good for themselves must first give it to others. Let their very existence be a blessing to others.

When such people are in harmony with all others, they are then perfectly attuned to the universal creative consciousness power *and they are brought into the flow of the Father 'nature' which is growth, protection, nourishment (physical, mental, spiritual) healing, fulfillment of need, within a system of law and order.*

How can I describe for you, my inner glow, my transcendent brightness and brilliance of joy and powerful feelings of love which possessed and inflated my entire being with their intensity until I cried out with the pressure within my mind and heart. *It was so powerful it seemed it would entirely dissolve my bodily form. As I received all this supreme, sublime understanding of the Reality, our Source of Being,* *and the true nature of creation itself – and of mankind, I was uplifted in spirit and my body became light as air.*

*At that time, when I was thus elevated within the **Divine Creative Power Itself,** I was indeed almost a 'Divine Person' myself, experiencing a high degree of the **'Nature'** of the **'Father-Creative Power'** within me and feeling Its own drive and caring concern for all humanity. Therefore, I could later say with truth: **"Only I know and have seen the 'Father'."***

In that moment how I yearned to teach, heal, comfort, uplift, feed, take away the people's pain and misery.

I longed to release them from their fear of a mythical 'avenging god'!

*When I returned to tell them the truth, How I would emphasize the **'reality'** of the **'Father-Creative Power'** – **PERFECT LOVE** – supplying their every need. All they had to do was 'Ask, seek, knock' and all their needs – of whatever kind – would be bestowed upon them.*

How joyously I would tell them the 'good news' that 'redemption from suffering' lay within their grasp if they only took the necessary steps to cleanse their minds and hearts of the TWIN IMPULSES of manifested 'being'.

This should be simple enough, I thought, one only needed understanding and self-control.

(I have descended towards your vibrations to refer back to my actual state of mind during the time I was in the desert. It will help your own understanding immeasurably if you try to enter my 'state of consciousness' at that time. So many things, such as

*my works of healing and 'walking on water' will become clear to you. They will be seen to be a natural consequence of my new understanding of the **'Father-Creative Power'**.*

If you read the gospels of Matthew and Mark, their records will have new meaning for you.)

*To return to my final hours of enlightenment, – there I was in the desert, possessing the clear understanding that man himself – (through no fault of his own) creates the barrier to attunement to the **'Father-Creative Power'**, and now I was longing to hurry back and teach, heal, comfort, dry the tears of those I so greatly pitied.*

Yet I was reluctant to leave this 'hallowed' place where I had been so illumined and transformed in spirit. On the other hand, what a wonderful future lay ahead of me!

I would walk through all the cities, towns, villages and tell everyone I met – the GOOD NEWS! 'The Kingdom of Heaven', that place where all sickness disappeared and every need was supplied was within them! Because I knew that the 'Father' and I were 'one', now that my mind had been cleansed of the old thoughts and ideas, I would direct healing at their illness and disease. I would teach them how to relieve their poverty.

*When the **FATHER CONSCIOUSNESS** within me began to dim, and I gradually returned to human consciousness I became aware of gnawing hunger and also a return of my human conditioning and thought.*

My reactions to my six weeks' experiences began to change. My usual human awareness of 'me' and my desires, took over my thoughts.

'Why, the most amazing and completely unexpected thing has happened to me!' I exulted. 'I have been given knowledge beyond any yet given to any other man.'

I was jubilant with the realization that, at last, my doubt and rebelliousness against the avenging 'god' of the Traditional Orthodox Jews was vindicated. I had been right after all!

Who had ever suspected the human mind could be so highly creative, that a strongly-held thought or desire would actually manifest itself in the visible realm? I realized that Moses must have known something of this, because he had accomplished some strange things when the Israelites were in dire need.

He became a leader and changed the course of the Israelites previously enslaved in Egypt. I could return now and free my people from the rigid control of their own Teachers.

My hunger pains now became intense. It occurred to me that I could turn stones into bread to satisfy my longing for food because I remembered that the **'Father-Creative Power'** *worked through my mind and therefore, everything in the universe would be subject to my command.*

I was about to speak the 'word' which would change stones into bread but something in me halted me abruptly.

It came to me, strongly, that the **'Father-Creative Conscious-ness'** *was perfect protection, nourishment, fulfillment of need, and so the hunger would be taken care of, if I asked the 'Father' for relief.*

I realized that if the little 'i', the human me, in my need, used the 'Creative power' for selfish reasons, I would be erecting a barrier between the 'Father-Creative Consciousness' and myself, and everything I had just learnt might well be taken away from me.

This frightened me, and swiftly I asked the **'Father-Creative Power'** *for new strength to carry me back to habitations and Nazareth again.* **I also asked for relief of hunger in the form that would be right for me.** *Immediately, the hunger pangs subsided and I felt a surge of energy flow through my entire body. Thus, I proved that all I had seen, heard and understood was* **'reality'** *and not some vain imagining born of my time in the desert, fasting and alone.*

My new energy enabled me to make haste over the rough tracks on my way out of the desert.

On the way, I met a well-dressed man of sweet and pleasing countenance. He greeted me warmly, expressing concern on seeing my rough, unkempt appearance and loss of condition.

Gladly, he sat me down on a rock and shared his excellent meat and bread with me. I wondered why he was in such a desolate place and where he had come from. In response to my questioning, he only smiled and seemed not the least surprised when I said I had been in the desert for so many days I had lost count of time. I explained how I was enlightened as to the true nature of the Creator of the world and shown the natural **Laws of Existence**. *He only smiled and nodded.*

'I am going back to my people to teach them everything I have learnt.' I said joyously. 'Why I will be able to heal them and bring them release from every sickness and trouble.'

The stranger replied sadly: 'It will take many millennia.'

I was about to rebuke his lack of faith when I realized he was gone.

I knew then that a Divine messenger had come to succor with good bread and meat – and compassionately give me warning that I might not find my mission so simple, despite my enthusiasm. I was deflated by his word of warning. My enthusiasm waned. The way to the first village on my road seemed endless. How a change in human thought produces a change of mood!

*It came to me that I could further prove the truth of all I had been shown by jumping over the edge of a precipice which would greatly shorten my journey. As I was about to do this, it came to me forcibly that I was trying to 'prove' my time of enlightenment was real. If I required such proof, then I was in a state of doubt and I would probably kill myself, besides I had been shown that in every eventuality I could lift my thoughts up to the **'FATHER-CREATIVE CONSCIOUSNESS'** and ask for a solution to every problem. How quickly I forgot the **Truth!***

So, I prayed, passionately asking forgiveness for being weak enough to indulge my own fantasies and seeking my own way of doing things.

Again, the answer came in renewed strength and a greater sureness of foot as I scrambled over the rough ground. I found, too, that I was covering long distances so quickly that it seemed that I had stepped outside normal time reckoning, and I was in a lighter dimension where human experience was lifted above its heavy thralldom of exhausting expenditure of energy.

Walking was so easy it was now invigorating. I exulted in the fact that I had found the key to 'more abundant life'!

A while later, feeling so much at ease, my mind began to wander and I thought about my meeting with the stranger and the kindness he had shown me. But I also remembered his warning and again my old nature re-asserted itself and I felt deeply rebellious that he should presume to tell me how my work would go. I decided he knew nothing about my future and set his warning aside.

'Why,' I thought, 'with my knowledge I could accomplish things no man has ever done before. Instead of struggling in a difficult life, I could begin to accumulate wealth easily, attract followers wherever I went, and share my knowledge with them to make their lives easier also. I could take away all pain and suffering.'

As I contemplated the many places I could visit so easily, I felt myself skimming the surface of the ground and rising until I reached the highest peak of a steep mountain overlooking the countryside below.

There it was, all laid out before me. I felt my previous enthusiasm return. Why, it would be so simple to round up the people and share all my knowledge with them. I would become powerful, even famous as the man who rescued mankind from all their sickness and troubles. I would gain their admiration and respect and would no longer be remembered as an idle worthless fellow.

With a tremendous shock, all I had been taught so recently, but a few hours ago, returned to mind with great force and clarity.

Had I not been taught that the only way I could ever prosper was to abandon my self-will and turn to the 'FATHER' for assistance in everything I undertook?

Then I remembered that creation had its own special purposes to fulfill. The individualizing process had created the 'pull and push', the 'give and take' in human behavior. Although these human characteristics caused people great anguish in their lives, was it not the anguish which forced them to seek better ways to live in order to find true happiness? I realized that the ills of mankind had their place in the human scheme of existence.

Was it right for me to bring privileged information to people in order to nullify the effects of the 'individualizing process'?

I realized I had been thinking from the 'central point' of my individuality, the 'ego', and it was the ego drive which built barriers between mankind and 'Father-Creative Consciousness'. Therefore, my 'Central point of human desiring' would have to be conquered if I was to live in perfect harmony with my 'Father' as was my sincere intention.

And so I continued on my way, pondering what might lie ahead and how I might best overcome the impulses governing my humanhood in order to remain in the Flow of 'Father Consciousness' from which I would draw inspiration, guidance, answers to problems, my daily nourishment, daily health, daily protection. In fact, I realized that whilst I remained within this daily Flow of Father Consciousness', no harm could ever come near me and my every need would be met. And more importantly: the 'Father Consciousness' working through me would do whatever was required for people in dire need of healing and comfort.

At all times, I must overcome my rebelliousness against the harsh realities of existence and listen to the 'inner voice' and conform to the 'Higher Will' of the 'Father'. This 'Higher Will' was 'Perfect Love' directed entirely at promoting my highest good. It would be extremely foolish, I realized, to continue along the path of 'self-will' which had dictated my behavior to that time.

It was then that I was inspired to speak in parables to the people. Those who were ready to receive the knowledge would understand and make good use of it.

*But, as it turned out, even my disciples could not rid themselves sufficiently of Jewish doctrine to enable them to understand either the principle of consciousness or the activity of the **Divine 'Creative Power'** within creation. (Until this time, it has remained a mystery to all except the spiritually enlightened.)*

*Even the spiritual words of enlightenment cannot be immediately, fully comprehended by the human mind; therefore, these **Letters** must be read slowly and accompanied by much meditation and prayer to be properly understood.*

*Remember, unless you can become as a '**child**' – (getting rid of a useless clutter of beliefs, prejudices, resentments, ambitions, and ego-drive) with a mind filled with wonder and utmost faith, you will not be able to absorb these pages as you should.*

To become a 'child', you must make an effort to shed all past mental conditioning. If you are mentally/emotionally/ physically suffering, it is only because whatever have been your most sincere beliefs, they have not been helpful to you; they have not promoted your well-being.

*It is time to examine your **MINDSET**. Are you happy with it?*

You can make choices, and as you make them, you can call upon the 'Father' to help you make the changes, and the help will surely be given you, – providing you do not doubt.

I therefore urge you to continue to read and absorb the following pages. I want to impress on you the strength of your mindset – which is the sum total of all your conscious and subconscious programming.

It is essential you should understand that none of this human mindset has its origins in the spiritual dimension.

It is entirely earthly and probably filled with mythical ideas, prejudices, misconceptions, resentments, buried memories of past hurts, and habitual methods of dealing with the ups-and-downs of life. Your human mindset (including any religious ideas or beliefs) determines your world, your relationships, experiences, successes, failures, happiness and misery. It is even responsible for your sickness, disease and accidents. Nothing happens by chance. Everything is woven out of the inner threads of your personal consciousness – thoughts, expectations, beliefs in life, fate, "God". You live in a world of your own making. This is why children raised in the same environment turn out differently. Each one has its own individual Mindset constructed according to inherent character traits.[69]

This "Letter" continues with a high-level explanation of elements of Consciousness. The "Letters" are constructed in way that slowly builds your understanding of the new knowledge you will gain. Read them slowly and accompany your reading with meditation and prayer to properly understand them. The next excerpt continues to develop your knowledge by providing a conceptual explanation of consciousness and individuality, before the "Letters" shift their focus onto more scientific explanations consistent with our current (-day) scientific understandings.

Excerpt Three:

Light Individualized

> *It has been said of me that 'my body rose from the dead'. What an absurdity conjured up by earthly minds which were at a loss to satisfactorily explain my death as a felon on a cross!*
>
> *What need would I have of an earthly body to continue existence in the next dimension?*
>
> *How could such a ridiculous myth persist even into the 21ˢᵗ century? It has been a measure of the lack of understanding of 'Christians' that they have blindly accepted such a dogma to this very time.*
>
> *Think about this carefully. Having been released from an earthly body and after my experience of the ecstasy and glorious rapture of passing into a higher dimension of **UNIVERSAL CONSCIOUSNESS**, why would I want to return to the earthly dimension to enter my body again? Of what use would it be to me in your world or in mine? Whilst the 'physical substance' of my body might be spiritualised when perfectly attuned to the '**Father Love Consciousness**' whilst I still lived on earth, would not my body*

be an encumbrance and a deterrent to my subsequent journeys within the highest Spiritual Kingdoms? Visible things are but a manifestation of specific frequencies of vibration in consciousness which produces a 'SHIMMER OF MOTES OR PARTICLES' giving an appearance of solid 'matter'.

Each visible substance possesses its own unique vibrational frequency. A change in the rate of vibration produces a change in the appearance of 'matter'. As consciousness energies change so do the appearances of 'matter' change.

Therefore, it was possible for me to focus and lower my frequencies of consciousness to that point where my form became visible to the human eye. I could return to my disciples and be seen by them. And I did so. I loved them more than ever before, and owed them as much comfort and support as I was able to give them after my death. Not only this, it was necessary to direct my own power into their minds in order to give them the impetus and courage to continue the work I had started.

*However, I want you to know that the 'individualised consciousness' which has ascended in vibrational frequencies to the very portals of the **Universal Creative Dimension** becomes **LIGHT INDIVIDUALISED**, an **INDIVIDUALISED CONSCIOUSNESS** which needs no body in which to express and enjoy all that the **GLORIOUS CONSCIOUSNESS** can devise in the highest **SPIRITUAL REALMS**. It is a supreme and enraptured state of being having none of the needs, desires, impulses experienced by those who have not fully mounted high beyond and above the ego.*

Whilst living on earth, your minds remain anchored within certain parameters of vibrational frequencies, imprisoned in bodies which have their own needs. If your consciousness were to truly soar beyond these parameters, your earthly self would disappear. When I was trapped in a body, I was also largely confined to these parameters of vibrational frequencies and consciousness.

Furthermore, imagination alone can soar no further than your previous experiences and therefore you are confined to your past which you project into your future.

However – little by little – you will be led by those minds which are sensitive enough to access the higher spiritual dimensions and can thus move beyond your present consciousness boundaries. They will record for you those wondrous experiences and states of being beyond your own, to which you yourselves will then be able to aspire. In this way, you go forwards in levels or steps of spiritual development.

Each step brings you a higher vision of what can be achieved and out of this vision you formulate a new goal. With this goal ever before you, you work to cleanse yourself of the contaminating influence of the 'bonding-rejection' impulses of your earthly existence. Step by step you transcend your ego.

*When you transcend your ego and it dies within your consciousness, you are now abundantly alive within the **'Father Love Consciousness'** and find the reality of the kingdom of heaven in your lives, within yourself and in your environment.*

*To enable YOU to reach these pinnacles of love, joy, harmony and rapture, I lived, worked and died in Palestine and I have come to you now in these **Letters.***

Let not my work be in vain this second time. As you read these pages, seek, meditate and pray for inspiration, you will come to feel the 'Father's' response and if you listen every day attentively, you will hear the 'Father's' Voice.

This Voice is ever with you. Dismantle the barriers created by self-will. Open yourselves to receive strength, power, inspiration and love direct from the 'Father Love Consciousness'.

*Read and re-read these **Letters** that they may eventually become absorbed into your consciousness. As you do so, you will be journeying towards **LIGHT**, and you will radiate **LIGHT** to others. Such **LIGHT** is not just 'light' as is electricity but is the very nature of **UNIVERSAL CONSCIOUSNESS** which I described to you in my **Letter 1**.*

*Therefore, as you radiate the **LIGHT**, you will radiate unconditional love. You will promote the growth and spiritual development of every other living entity. You will yearn to nourish and nurture, you will work to promote protection and healing and education. You will long to assist in the establishment of loving law and order in which all will be able to live harmoniously, successfully and prosperously. **You will be in the Kingdom of Heaven.***[70]

The next excerpt comes later in the "Letters" as they transition to topics regarding modern science.

Excerpt Four:

Throwing Down the Gauntlet

Therefore, it is absolutely necessary for me to refute some of the 'scientific theories' and show them to be as erroneous as are the so-called 'truths' of Christian Doctrine. In arriving at some of these 'theories', scientists and churchman alike have dipped into the realms of unproven preposterous suppositions to answer questions which have previously been unanswerable by the earthly mind only.

*Having told you that the substance of your material world is basically electrical particles agitated at high speed within 'space', your science is unable to tell you '**why**' such 'energy particles' take on the density and form of 'matter' except to speak of forces of fusion which happen to create the elements.*

*Science cannot tell you what is the '**Motivating Force**' which draws particles into the form of elements.*

Neither can science tell you from whence such energy particles originally came except to say that they were released during the time of the Big Bang which they believe gave the first impetus to creation.

Why a sudden 'Big Bang' – of what? What was the Motivating Factor behind it?

Science speaks about electromagnetism but cannot say from whence come such energies which appear and disappear. Where do they go? Why do they come back? From the human perspective, there appears to be no intelligible activity within or behind its work.

Science says that electromagnetism 'just is' – a simple fact of existence – yet it produces highly purposeful and intelligent work in the form of millions of billions of substances of which your universe is made. How does this happen?

There is nothing that electromagnetism has brought into visible being which the human mind can deem to be lacking purpose or meaning.

Science ignores this most basic and vital level of creation. Without an answer to this question, as to why everything which has been brought into visible manifestation by the activity of the twin energies of electromagnetism is invariably purposeful, successful and rational – nothing of any value in the search for your origins will be discovered.

*Until science can probe and discover the '**Reality**' of the '**space**' in which electrical particles of 'visible being' are supported, science will forever remain behind locked doors of materialism. It will be barred to eternal Truth and universal wisdom and imprisoned within the bondage of reason alone – reason which is solely the product of the finite activity of brain cells.*

*It is to the **true nature** of the **SPACE** I intend to introduce you – but before proceeding to this, I must first bring many highly pertinent questions to your attention.*

Down the ages, much of the work produced by electromagnetism has appeared to the mind, vision and touch of living entities as being solid, unchangeably durable. Metals, wood, rocks, living entities were all believed to be composed of solid, inanimate or living 'matter'. With such a belief in a solid universe it is only natural that the mystical prophets of old should have envisaged a 'Mighty Individual' possessing enormous powers in creating all the solid substances of the universe. In visualising such a 'Mighty Individual', it was only natural they should perceive a 'Kingly' figure of universal control, possessing a retributive nature when confronted with the behaviour of mankind which

created a turbulent society. Neither Prophets of old nor science of today has been near to the Truth of Existence.
Both have completely missed the truth.

*Science says that life began when in some unexplained way, a **correct** combination of chemical reactions produced a molecule capable of making copies of itself by triggering further chemical reactions. Such a description of the enormous and teeming complexity and power of the **LIFE FORCE as being discernible because it is 'capable of replicating itself'**, reveals the basic impoverishment of scientific perception and thought which produced such a theory!*

Furthermore, the suggestion that such a combination of 'inanimate' chemicals could get together in a specific way – accidentally – to produce such an astounding result of 'self-replication' remains unquestioned scientifically.

This is because the finite human mind, even though scientific, cannot deal with such a strange eventuality of uninitiated 'self-replication'. It is too suggestive of a magical occurrence – of some intervention from an unimaginable source which scientific men dare not contemplate for fear of ridicule.

This sheep-like acquiescence is considered more scientific than producing 'inspired' theories blocked by the materialistic laws science has established for itself. This block to future scientific progress will prevent science properly investigating the realm of mind and spirit until some enlightened scientist defies convention and dares to cross the borderline between the 'seen' and the 'unseen'.

Prophets of old, if presented with the theory of molecular self-replication would have no difficulty with such a 'magical occurrence' and would say that 'God' made the chemical combinations and imbued them with life. That would not be the right explanation either.

It is this old religious concept of a 'God on High' 'creating from afar' which is blocking the man of science from moving forward to more spiritually aware reflections. Therefore, despite science's seeming emancipation from age-old doctrines, it is still as mentally bound and hindered by fears of ancient shibboleths as in the 19th century. It adopts its ridiculous theories because it has not yet perceived the **'Reality'** *of* **Our Source of Being** *behind and within the living molecule.*

Continuing its story of creation, *science states that after the 'self-manufacture' of living molecules capable of replicating themselves, they 'formed themselves' into a living cell (so small it cannot be seen by the naked eye), which became the building block for all the multiplexity of living organisms, including plants, insects, reptiles, birds, animals and man himself. Therefore, all living things have a common ancestor – the first living molecule.*

Science cannot explain why the self-replicating molecules combined themselves into a living cell. It remains a mystery to science to this day.

The living cell, your science tells you, is endlessly repeated in a billion-billion-billion differing forms. It is the building block of the visible universe. How can this be? What impulse motivates such replication? Science cannot say. Entrenched in its own blindness, it has dragged people down into materialistic blindness with it.

*And now – the first living cell deserves the undivided attention of anyone seriously seeking the spiritual dimension and the **'Mainspring of Existence'** – because the first living molecule and the first living cell are the very first evidence of some **intelligent activity** within 'matter' – within the universe.*

The foremost feature displaying sense and sensibility is the function of the membrane which covers the cell, giving it protection and individuality. Think about this 'miraculous' phenomenon.

The cell takes in, from the environment, only selected nourishment through the membrane.

Not only does the cell take in the right nutrition but – having utilised the nutrition – the cell rids itself of the waste through the permeable membrane.

You should ask yourself how the 'purely physical' membrane of the cell, invisible to your eye, can 'distinguish and select' the correct nourishment to enhance its well-being and then exercise sufficient discernment to rid itself of unwanted toxic matter?

*Do you not see a high degree of **purposefulness** within all this activity and can you believe that such purposefulness is accidental?*

*And is not **PURPOSE** the very hallmark of **Intelligence?***

*Not only this, the membrane of the cell continues to do this work of selection of nutrition and discarding of waste in a billion-billion different circumstances and conditions relating to survival within differing species and differing environments. Is this not evidence of **PURPOSEFULNESS** displayed within* *every single action of every single species be it insects, plants, reptiles, birds, animals and human beings?*

Could you not describe the universe as being the consistent and undeviating **IMPULSE** *of* **PURPOSEFULNESS** *made visible within the realm of visible 'matter'?*

Is the spirit of **PURPOSEFULNESS** *a physical element – or one of 'consciousness'?*

And if you can accept that **PURPOSEFULNESS** *is an undeniable creative impulse behind* **EXISTENCE**, *then can you move on to the next perception of your universe as being the visible manifestation of* **'an INTELLIGENT APPRAISAL of cause and effect'** *clearly evident within living 'matter'? For – if the living cell can select the right nourishment* **and also provide for the elimination of toxic waste** *– this simple activity displays an awareness of the need for digestion and also foresees the resultant build up of toxic waste, and the need for the elimination of such waste to ensure the continued health of the cell. Is this not a clear indication of* **an INTELLIGENT APPRAISAL of 'Cause and Effect'?**

Furthermore – Science says that the cell contains a 'nucleus' which might be likened to the brain of a human being since it conveys messages and its most important function is the storage of information, the 'library' which contains not just the details relating to one cell but of the whole body in which its resides!

In fact, on investigation by science, it would appear that the cell itself is a system of chemical 'messages' carried out in a purposeful, intelligent and intelligible way. How could this happen if the **origins** *of the cell's molecules were only* *inanimate chemical elements? Would you dispute that behind every 'messenger with a message to convey' there is intelligent thought or consciousness? And behold how accurate are the messages transferred from cell to cell to ensure the accurate replication of certain species for millions of years?*

At what point in creation then, did 'consciousness' creep into living organisms? And how did intelligent thought which weighs and decides come into the field of unconscious inanimate matter?

*Without inherent consciousness, how can so much informed and informing activity take place in a cell invisible to the living eye? Is not such activity the **product** of **consciousness/ awareness, proving the presence of 'intelligent' life in its lowest denominator?***

Furthermore, a single living cell, in the form of a bacterium, can move about on its own and live its own specialised, frequently exciting life within the environment – or – as a virus doing its deadly specialized work of attacking specific targets within living organisms. Alternatively, the cell may be fixed within an organism, carrying out its own highly important work of construction and maintenance of some part of the organism. Such work produces 'living material' exactly suited – and necessary – to the living organ on which it works – be it parts of the human body or of animal life, or plant – such as human toes and spleen, or animal fur and tusks, or fish scales and feathers of birds, or bark of tree and foliage on branches, or petals and stalk of flowers, or antennae of butterflies and their gauzy wings, the reptilian skin of crocodiles and their teeth, the eyes of squid and their skins which change colour according to need of camouflage. Each of these completely diverse and seemingly unrelated physical phenomena are created by the individual, specialised work of billions and billions and billions of identical living cells.

On contemplating the magnitude and diversity of the work accomplished by a simple living cell invisible to the naked eye – can you believe in a mechanistic universe?

It would be possible to do so, if the 'matter' produced by such cells was illogical, offering no plausible purpose behind or reason for its existence – devoid of personal consciousness.

But this is not so. These identical living cells work together in harmony within man or beast, **to make a liver** *with its multiple duties within a body,* **to create an intricate eye** *having its own specific purposes of putting the entity into direct and intelligent touch with its environment, incorporating the assistance of the brain,* **or strong bones** *expressly and intricately designed in conjunction with tendons and muscles, to unite with others in such convenient ways as to enable full and supple movement of the entity. Furthermore, the cells never intrude on each other's work.*

When creating a kidney, they do not suddenly make an ear.

When creating hair they do not suddenly launch into making skin. No, cells create the scalp and the selfsame cells create the hair. The only difference between skin and hair cells is the work they do, second by second, throughout a lifetime. Why?

What is the 'Motivating and Inspiring Factor'? Accident?

What organising **intelligence** *set the entire process of creation in motion from the most fundamental level of the formation of simple elements out of free electrical particles within 'space',*

the combining of elements to form chemicals, the correct com-
bination of specific chemicals to form a living molecule, the
correct combination of living molecules to make a living cell
which can take in nutrition, excrete waste, build according to
clear-cut specifications, move about, and **sustain** *this enor-*
mous edifice of creation consistently through billions of years?

*Not only this, but what is the '****Motivating Force****' which has*
designed and successfully evolved within living systems and
entities, billions and billions of different ways in which to
fertilise seeds of every kind – whether they be those of plants,
insects, reptiles, birds, animals or human beings, evolving for
each an intelligent system of procreation suited to climatic
conditions, the production of vegetation in the environment,
in order to ensure survival?

Is not SURVIVAL also evidence of intelligent purposeful
activity?

And having accomplished this great feat of creativity, should
you not question how it is that every living species has its own
individualistic way of rearing its young and protecting it as
far as possible until the young are capable of **SURVIVAL** *on*
their own? Is this not **LOVE FOR CREATION** *active in its*
highest form?

You cannot move on from this analysis of what the human
intelligence has to say about the origins of life and creativity,
*without mentioning the '****all important molecules DNA****'*
– which are said to carry the 'plan' for the whole organism
– plant or baby. Furthermore, these DNA molecules give
the instructions to the cells, informing them they shall build
according to the chromosomes deposited by the seed.

*Yes, indeed, in place of **Intelligence** – science has given you the **DNA molecules** as your source of existence, your supreme leader, your director of creation upon which materialistic, flimsy cells, the whole of creation must depend for its survival. Behold the glorious **DNA – Lord of your creation!***

*From whence did the DNA cells draw their **intelligent directional powers?***

*Science is quite satisfied now that it has been able to satisfactorily explain why the various species of every kind replicate themselves so accurately and consistently. **Science would have you believe that you live in a purely mechanistic universe; that the phenomenon of evolution arises out of chance mutations and the 'survival of the fittest'.***

If you study the various organisms of creation, the multifold and differing activities of related species, can you truly believe in such an unlikely materialistic concept?

*It has been no mere coincidence that, today, to enable you to discover the vast **Intelligence** behind creation, you have numerous creative people who embark on difficult journeys to explore, determine and photograph the habitats and habits of wild creatures and plants. You are entertained – and instructed – by a feast of facts and photographs of the **wonders** of your universe.*

*In my time on earth, I had no such marvels to refer to in order to teach the Jews the universal **Truth of Existence**. I only had domestic animals and birds to use as examples of the marvellous inventiveness and intelligence and **awareness** apparent in every living thing. Nowhere has it been written* *in the gospels that I referred to a High and Mighty Jehovah as Creator as was customary with the Jewish Leaders.*

*No, I turned to the countryside, the flowers and birds and tried to show my fellow countrymen that they were surrounded by a marvelous and miraculous creation. Two thousand years ago in your dimension, we lacked your modern scientific background to be able to intelligently observe and explain the activity of what I termed the '**Father**' everywhere around them.*

*To discover your true **SOURCE of BEING**, I ask you to take stock of the unimaginable and indescribable complexity and diversity of purposeful work plainly evident in penguins and pigs.*

Can the human mind replicate any of the most basic of activities within – say – the digestive system, which swiftly summons up the requisite enzymes and hormones necessary for digestion.

How dare the finite mind, which is incapable of perceiving clearly the true creative process governed by instinctual knowledge, presume to state unequivocally – defying contradiction – that it understands the true origins of creation and the forces out of which creation took form?

What arrogance! These men can only think according to what their eyes tell them.

I view the present scientific ignorance with loving compassion, a degree of amusement, and a great all-consuming passion to puncture their pride. For until someone can penetrate their self-satisfaction and position of infallibility, a true mating of

Eternal Verities and human scientific knowledge can never take place. But it must take place; otherwise human spiritual evolution will remain at a standstill.

The scientific mind is too full of 'finitely' devised book lore, accepted formulas and equations, and the need for their fellows' approval, to permit mystical penetration by Higher Intelligences.

*On my behalf, I ask readers of these **Letters**, to form an association to challenge Science and ask 'at what point in the evolution of the 'material' world' is **CONSCIOUSNESS** first discernible?*

I repeat and mean what I say: Ask the scientist at what point in the evolution of the world is 'consciousness' first discernible. In the living cell? If in the living cell, ask whether it was discernible in the living molecules which combined to make a cell and encase itself in such an intelligently designed membrane, permitting the intake of selected food and excretion of toxic waste? How does it recognise toxic waste? And if it should be conceded that consciousness might be present in living molecules, should you not ask whether the chemical properties which became a living molecule might not themselves have possessed 'consciousness' which eventually impelled and propelled them into the life-giving combination to make a molecule? And having gone back thus far into the origins of existence – the chemical properties – you must still question why 'consciousness' should only become a viable presence within the chemicals – why not within the elements in which individuality first took shape, and if in the elements why should it be denied that 'consciousness' propels the electrical particles to form the elements? Is it rational to deny such a possibility?

And having reached such a possibility, should you not go farther and ask from whence comes electromagnetism? **What is the 'reality' of electricity more than streaks of fierce light now described by science as photons and electrons?**

And what is the 'reality' of magnetism more than two-fold energies of 'bonding and rejection' – energy impulses which have brought stability and order into chaos?

Ask science: "From whence comes electromagnetism which is responsible for the most basic steps in the creation of an ordered and orderly universe of an unimaginable complexity and diversity?"

I will now attempt to put into your words **THAT WHICH** *is beyond all words and presently beyond all 'individualised earthly comprehension'. Therefore, the intellect, although it assists the brain to understand, intellectually, the spiritual realities I am putting before you, it also creates a barrier to true spiritual perception and experience.*

For this reason, regard the following references to the **ULTI-MATE UNIVERSAL DIMENSION** *as only guidelines – ideas, 'shadow consciousness forms' of the* **REALITY** *behind and within your universe. ((Take each IDEA – one by one – into meditation))*

What I am about to explain is entirely within and of CONSCIOUSNESS without parameters and boundaries. If you are sufficiently spiritually evolved to follow me there, beyond the words, you will begin to understand 'spiritually' all I am trying to tell you. The words will guide you towards – and then unlock new 'vistas of being' for you.

Persevere! The **LIGHT** *will gradually, perhaps imperceptibly, penetrate your mind and you will have little bursts of insight.*

There are many who have experienced a little 'burst of insight', have briefly felt a touch of 'Divine Consciousness' and then, hardly daring to continue to believe in such a transcendent moment of awareness, have begun to question, doubt and finally dispel the little inflow of 'Divine Consciousness'. **Beware you do not do this.** *Disbelief will set you back, enmesh you in the material plane of existence more than you will ever know.*

Whatever you are given and able to receive – hold fast to it and do not doubt.

Doubt destroys steady progress because it creates its own 'consciousness forms' which will suppress and even eradicate the insight you had gained previously.

Therefore, your choice of thoughts – belief or disbelief, doubt or faith – construct or destroy your progress in your search for TRUTH.

Any denial erases from your consciousness the progress which has been previously made. Furthermore, the higher you ascend in spiritual truth, the more powerful do your thoughts become. Therefore, create and hold fast to your own spiritual momentum and allow no one to intrude and undermine that momentum. Hold firm to your former perceptions. In times of doubt, cruise along in positive thoughts, using enlightening affirmations, clinging to earlier inspirational guidance when your consciousness frequencies of vibration were higher. By use of your willpower, choosing affirmations containing 'golden nuggets' of spiritual Truth, return to this higher level of consciousness again and again. Do not, through mental laziness, wholly surrender to the ebb and flow of spiritual consciousness energies and become a spiritual 'see-saw'.

I cannot emphasize this danger of self-obstruction strongly enough. Become actively aware of it.

If you know anything of the accounts of my life in Palestine, you will recall that I, too, suffered the phenomenon of ebb and flow of spiritual consciousness and found it necessary to absent myself in the hills to pray and meditate and renew my spiritual strength.

*Therefore, understand your 'dry' periods, but do not give way to them by yielding passively to an undesirable change in your attitudes and mental/emotional patterns. As you conscientiously draw upon your **Source of Being** for new strength and the upliftment of your consciousness frequencies, so will these negative periods be greatly reduced in strength and duration.*

I repeat, at all times beware how you use your minds! Let your mental activity always be constructive that it may contribute to your own spiritual growth rather than its constant hindrance.[71]

The "Letters" continue with the story of creation; from the state prior to the Big Bang; the reason for the Big Bang; and the billions of years it took to create the material world; and from the most fundamental level of the formation of simple elements out of free electrical particles within "space;" to the most advanced entity in the universe—humankind itself.

In Part V of this book, I share the remaining steps of the seven-step process, along with my personal insights and the experiences I had while learning and undergoing the work necessary to cleanse my consciousness and spiritualize my mental processes; thereby changing the course of my life.

PART V

YOU CHOOSE YOUR PATH, DELIBERATELY OR BY DEFAULT

I see now that the circumstances of one's birth are irrelevant.
It is what you do with the gift of life
that determines who you are.

—Unknown

Chapter 9

CONCLUSION: PERSONAL INSIGHTS AND EXPERIENCES

Darkness cannot drive out darkness; only light can do that.
Hate cannot drive out hate; only love can do that.[72]
—Martin Luther King, Jr.

Please note:

- First: I have written this chapter assuming that you have read all the "Letters" and have a cursory understanding of the Truth of Existence; the Secrets of Creation; the required existence of the two fundamental, eternal, undeviating "impulses of creative being;" the Laws of Existence; and the many other concepts, mechanisms, and processes from which our Universe was created and that we use minute by minute to create and shape

171

our lives. The ideas discussed below probably will be foreign to you the first time you read through this book cover to cover. However, after you have completed Steps One and Two, the information discussed below will make more sense to you.

- Second: Throughout this Chapter, I refer to *Truth* or *Truths* with a capital *T.* This is done in order to be consistent with the teachings in the "Letters." *Truth* (or *Truths*) refers to many things, including, but not limited to: the truth of existence, the secrets of creation, the reality behind and within existence, the nature and existence of the Universal and the Divine, the twin impulses of being, and the laws of existence, to name a few. After reading the "Letters," understanding the information presented, and learning the lessons being taught, you too may accept these learnings as *Truths.*

And,

- Third: The Universal, the Divine, IT, Father, Father-Mother-Life, and Source of all Being are Terms used throughout the following pages. On your first read through of this material, consider them *interchangeable.* I have used these terms for two reasons:
  - The terms and where they are used within this chapter keep the text consistent with the "Letters," and
  - There are important and subtle differences that will become apparent to you after reading the "Letters" in their entireties. On your first read-through of this chapter, however, these differences are not important to your overall conceptual understanding.

You now know, both from science and from reading the "Letters," that there is nothing solid under the sun. Everything is composed of energy particles. All things that seem solid to the human senses— plants, wood, rocks, and animals—are composed of energy particles vibrating at a particular frequency. As the frequency of these energy particles changes, so does *the appearance* of that thing. Your *consciousness* affects the vibration of these energy particles directly. You and you alone shape the fabric of your consciousness with your thoughts and emotions. Remember, "You *think* with electrical impulses in the brain. You *feel* with magnetic impulses in your nervous system. They center and bond the electrical impulses into a cohesive whole."[73] Christ tells us, "You are not victims of fate – you are victims of your own creative consciousness until you realise that your consciousness is entirely of your own shaping."[74] You and I cannot escape the process of consciousness. We spin our human consciousness fabric with our thoughts and emotions— our electrical and magnetic impulses—to create a *lifeform*, a *blueprint* of our future experiences. The blueprint we each create is "an electrical outline of [our] intention [or desire or purpose] and the corresponding magnetic field of emotion draws particles of energy together to bring this driving intention [or desire or purpose] into visible manifestation."[75]

This creation in the unseen around you is *yours*. You create each of these blueprints, and the eventual manifestation of each brings into your experience both "its happy side and its dark side."[76] This book is intended (and designed) to help you learn how to gain control of your life and ascend in consciousness through teaching you how to create positive, life-giving consciousness forms.

For me, winning the Lexus convertible was an example of the happy side of the laws of existence. That Lexus showing up in my life was a direct result of me creating a lifeform, a blueprint of my desires. The corresponding emotions of joy, fun, and pride of ownership drew particles of energy together, bringing my focused intention into visible manifestation. Recall that each day for a year, I spent two to four minutes, fifteen to twenty times a day, imagining the experience of owning that Lexus. I sat quietly in my chair and imagined myself driving that car, reinforcing that blueprint. My emotional investment in imagining (in living technicolor) my top-down, wind-in-my-hair, joyous ride along the coast road strengthened the electromagnetic energies. Unbeknownst to me, I was creating this lifeform and magnetizing its manifestation into a future experience. This is a Universal Law—the law of cause and effect. This is a Truth.

The darker expression of these same laws? Me at the kitchen table crafting that suicide note. This darker side was a direct result of my consistent negative and selfish thoughts and emotions over many years. My personal consciousness created my experiences, my personal situations, and my financial issues. My thoughts and reactions to life drove my emotions and worked as a "feedback loop" to drive and reinforce more "doom and gloom" in thought and experience, strengthening the corresponding blueprints. My ego was firmly in control. My soul was "bound down within its secret dwelling place."[77]

The mental chains and thongs that I created and reinforced as I matured into adulthood (and continued to strengthen with every passing year) kept my soul trapped and my psyche burdened. (If you cannot remember what "mental chains" and "thongs" are, I refer you back to "Letter 1"). Finally, I reached that "fork in the road"—one path led to suicide, the other, as it turned out, to enlightenment, spiritual growth, and freedom. As I've shared, by that time I had come across *Christ's "Letters."* They gave me a glimmer of hope and inspired me—so, I took that path, not knowing where it would lead. With consistent study, practice, and a growing understanding, the knowledge and instructions (combined with the required work) shared in the "Letters" revolutionized my life, bringing me deep peace, joy, and love.

Not everyone will understand these Truths. We must each grow individually and come into the light. This will happen for each of us when we are ready—in this lifetime or in a future lifetime. As Christ says, "Your true purpose in your spiritual journey, is to break free of the bondage of the ego and make ever more pure contact with DIVINE CONSCIOUSNESS. It is your eventual destiny to recognize ITS omnipresence both within yourself and throughout your daily activities."[78] When you can express the golden qualities of Divine Consciousness, consistently, to everything, at all times, and in all circumstances in your world, you will be creating a little *pocket (or oasis)* of Divine Love in your environment. This *pocket* of unconditional love is an area of wholeness on the Earth that does not dissolve. Christ tells us that "…as more and more people on earth strive to respond to darkness in this way … The darkness itself will be affected – it cannot be otherwise…."[79] And so, he says, the number of those striving to create a *New Era of Love and Peace* in the world will "…begin to increase and swell, and eventually the voices of the Divine will begin to enlighten the responses of those who are still unenlightened."[80] Slowly, humanity will adopt broad new ethics governing their behaviors expressing love, consideration, and kindness to all. This will stop the wars, the hate, the judgments, the condemnations, and will dissolve the multitude of divisions currently expressed daily, moment by moment, by much of humanity.

For those who are ready and open to new learning and new concepts, I introduce you to these teachings—and offer a process, with clear instructions that, if followed, can bring you new spiritual insights and transform your life. It will enable you to come into alignment with who you really are at the core of your being and achieve your true purpose in life. As noted, when this happens to a critical mass of people, humankind will come together and express through us everything that Father-Mother-Life is … we will give unconditional love to everyone and to everything. We will save our planet from human-driven annihilation, fulfill our true purpose, and create a *New Era of Love and Peace* throughout the world.

Remember I mentioned that my wife, Elizabeth, looks at life through rose-colored glasses? I can see now that I had labeled Elizabeth's attitudes about and perspectives on life inappropriately: Elizabeth may not be perfect, but she is a visible and real expression of someone who gives love to all. She has been a clear and consistent expression of many aspects of Divine Consciousness; even though she does not recognize it. Over the years (even though I did not realize it) she has been a shining example for me (I was not able at that time to emulate her *rose-colored worldview*). Today I understand her view and am truly grateful for her ongoing support as I navigate the path to cleanse my consciousness fully and express unconditional love to everything in my world and throughout the universe.

MY EXPERIENCES AS I FOLLOW THIS PATH

As I write this, it has been just over three years since I began this journey, utilizing the knowledge I gained to reach out and *contact the Divine* and to cleanse and re-build my consciousness. This *contact* takes place when you gain the knowledge and insights about the *Truth of Existence, Creation,* and the *twin impulses of being* and follow the instructions outlined in the "Letters." This process is outlined later in this chapter as Steps Two through Seven. A key component of the seven-step process—a specific, proper meditation technique—is included in the Steps. Prior to learning *how and why* to meditate (and, ultimately, for the meditation technique to be most successful), one must complete Steps Two through Five and then the corresponding lessons in order to correctly visualize the meanings of the words in the prayer you will learn (in the "Letters") to recite at the beginning of your meditation. Therefore, only after I had completed all the necessary learnings and steps was I able to reach out properly to make contact with the Divine.

When I first started meditating, as instructed in the "Letters," I felt nothing I recognized as *contact*. After a few months of meditating daily, I got in the swing of clearing my mind completely of the string of endless thoughts that flow non-stop into the human mind and permeate it (you are instructed how do to do this in the "Letters"). I persisted. After the first seven months, while meditating, I felt a small opening at the top of my head. This was followed by what I recognize now as an inflow of Father-Mother-Life into the crown of my head. The opening increased in size slowly over time.

In some meditations, I would experience (*feel*) contact with the Divine; in others, I would not. I *feel this contact* as an inflow of spiritual power, soft energy (if you will), slowly growing in both intensity and size. I reminded myself that during the times I did not *feel the contact*, it was because my spiritual frequencies were at a low ebb and as such I could not feel the vibrations of Divine Consciousness. However, Christ assures us in the "Letters" that "Although you may not feel them [vibrations of Divine Consciousness], rest assured that always you are enfolded in them and in DIVINE LOVE."[81] Remember, he says, that "…your true 'Spiritual Father-Mother' … radiates unstintingly and continually and consistently – UNCONDITIONAL PARENTING LOVE."[82] And so, undeterred and without doubt, I persisted. By the end of eleven months, the opening had grown and the inflow of Father-Mother-Life was so strong (and lasted well beyond the time in meditation) that I wondered initially if I had damaged my brain. This was nonsense, I decided, and continued.

Over time, when meditating, I felt Father-Mother-Life flow into either my head or my chest or down one side or both sides of my body. Then I began to have meditations in which Father-Mother-Life would flow into my head, into my chest, into my solar plexus and groin, and back up to my head. Sometimes, this traveling spiritual power was gentle and moved slowly. At other times, it was strong and moved rapidly up and down my body. Its location in my body varied. It would enter my head and stay centered there, or move into my chest or solar plexus, or be in all three places at once.

As I continued with daily meditations, daily cleansing, and the re-building of my consciousness, my contact with the Divine became clearer, beautiful, and more powerful.

(This happens slowly and imperceptibly, and "little by little, the darkness of the human ego is dissipated and is illumed by Divine Inspiration"[83] until you *feel* the contact.) The stronger the inflow of spiritual energy was, the more my body reacted in movements and vibrations. My head vibrated, oscillating rapidly side to side (this oscillation, measured against the center line of my nose, was a one-quarter-inch movement each way). Or, my chest expanded while simultaneously my back lifted off the chair, pressing my shoulders and buttocks into the chair. Sometimes my abdomen contracted and my body reacted as if it were doing a sit-up, lifting my head and shoulders off of the chair.

As I became more receptive to the inflow of spiritual power, I began to shift into higher frequencies of consciousness. At first these shifts were dramatic, rapid sideways oscillations of my head with step-like jolts into higher levels of consciousness. Many times, it felt like an engine revving up, requiring a shift into a higher gear on a manual transmission. But the gear shift lever was stuck, and the engine began to over-rev. Then either I shifted violently into a higher frequency (higher gear and lower rpms) or came back down (same gear with lower rpms) to a lower frequency.

After many months, these shifts became subtle and, many times, they were imperceptible. I can tell now when I move into a higher consciousness frequency, but I can't describe it to you because we don't have the human language to communicate this. But a telltale, knowable physical response is that I am barely breathing. To an outside observer it might look like I am experiencing a significant convulsive fit and should be rushed to the hospital. I am glad no one views these experiences, for not only would they likely be concerned for me, they would no doubt interrupt the magnificent and beautiful state of consciousness I am experiencing.

When I first started to experience these higher levels of consciousness, I did not have a private space. I did my meditations in the living room of our one-bedroom rental apartment. Elizabeth gave me privacy by staying in bed and reading her book. However, a few times she passed by the living room on her way to get a second cup of coffee and reported later that I'd had a wide, silly grin on my face. If you join me in this process, completing the learnings, learning how to meditate properly, and sticking with it, you too may enjoy these amazing and beautiful experiences yourself as you ascend in consciousness.

At the end of the first year of study and practice, I had an *experience* during two separate meditations, about five days apart. These *experiences* are incredibly hard to describe. The English language and human understanding and reasoning regarding life and existence lack the knowledge and ability to communicate fully what I experienced. It involved *the feelings* more than the intellect and brain cells. I can only describe the experience as follows:

> *I was enveloped, cradled, bathed in an absolute and complete feeling of Love. The inner peace, joy, and contentment was nothing, nothing like I had ever experienced in my life up to that moment. I felt that if I could remain in that state, I did not care what happened to my body, what ailments it had or what pain it experienced. I felt I was at one with my creator and my creator loved me regardless of my past transgressions. I wanted to remain in this state, but alas, I came out of my meditation, and the feeling slowly faded. Thankfully, the memory remains!*

At the end of my first year of study and consistent practice, my perceptions of Reality (both within me and surrounding me) became so clear and transcendent, the ground of my communication with other people changed radically. I could still communicate and enjoy the company of people, but what I now knew (and there being no one I could talk to about it) left me feeling mentally isolated and alone. After a few months, I reached out to one of my sisters. My sister was on her own spiritual journey, using teachings from a teacher of long ago. Therefore, I did not push my way or my new beliefs and understandings onto her, but I could at least talk peripherally to a receptive ear about what I was experiencing. This was helpful in alleviating some of my feelings of isolation.

I also reached out to a close friend, a Muslim, and invited him to read *Virus of the Mind* as his first step. He did. To guide him through the next steps of this seven-step process, I offered a process similar to the one in this book (albeit I offered each of the scientific books, one at a time, as titles for him to pre-read). When I finally introduced him to the "Letters," he was open to reading and learning. I shared the exact (and truncated) process outlined in this book with another friend, and he too is now reading the "Letters." These two experiences with friends assisted me in shaping the seven-step process outlined in this book. I believe that sharing this journey with other like-minded individuals is germane to completing the *Seven Steps* with ease. If you begin this journey, I welcome you to seek support by becoming a member of our online community. The shape, timing, and form of this online community will be announced on my website at *www.DNeilElliott.com*.

A Second Personal Experience

Several weeks ago, I had a meditation in which I felt and experienced unconditional love. It was not directed to me but was emanating from me—unconditional love for everyone and everything in my past and present, regardless of who they were/are, or what they did/do. I had never felt that before, for anyone; other than for my wife and children. However, the human expression of unconditional love is completely different. As I said earlier, with our human, limited, and materialized experience, language, and reasoning abilities, I cannot explain it properly or convey the emotion and feelings I experienced. Again, thankfully, the memory remains!

My meditations have slowly evolved over time as I have worked to cleanse my consciousness and rebuild it with my perceptions of the highest and best; the golden qualities of Divine Consciousness. My spiritual "dry periods" became less frequent, and the duration of those periods diminished. It takes consistent dedication to achieve the true purpose of your existence—your true goal in life—and to evolve both your consciousness and your reality. The goal is to achieve "*A constant and mutual* reciprocation of communication between the *Source of all Being* and creation."[84] and to express the *Divine* to everyone and everything in your environment; in your world. This constant and mutual reciprocation of communication is now a part of my everyday life. It is altogether beautiful, supportive, comforting, and peaceful. During my meditations, my awareness of IT is heightened, illuminating, and completely present and known to me. Another example of this transcendent, immeasurable, and ineffable experience is shared below (taken from my spiritual journal) through the use of an analogy that will hopefully give you a sense of its magnificence and beauty.

A Third Personal Experience

My meditation today (nearing three years of study, meditation, and prayer) was totally beautiful, peaceful, amazing, and comforting—and thoroughly indescribable! I will use an analogy to give you (the reader) a sense, a glimpse of the beauty, joy, love, and peace I experienced.

I settled down and finished giving thanks to my body; to every cell in my body and my mind. Before I finished giving thanks, I shifted into a high frequency of consciousness. I said the prayer, and then my mind cleared and an amazing and beautiful process began. I felt a beautiful, soft inflow of Father-Mother-Life into the top of my brain, and it slowly expanded to encompass all of my brain. I cannot explain this fully, but it was like (for lack of a better analogy) washing a bowl of grapes—where each grape is a brain cell, and Life force energy (the clean, fresh water flowing continually over and submerging the grapes) is soft, gentle, cool, and soothing; supporting, enveloping, and cradling every grape. This process was continuous and lasted the entire ninety minutes. It was— incredible! I felt loved unconditionally, comforted, supported, and cared for. It is a lasting memory that lingers, and the sensation and energy flow continues to last, at the time of writing this, six hours beyond the end of my meditation. It is Life affirming and utterly peaceful. It is radiant and rapturous joy and Love for the Source of our Being.

These learnings have changed my life. I no longer judge, condemn, or demean others in word, thought, or deed. I no longer feel jealousy, hate, or envy. I am at peace with the world and everything in it. I still judge for myself whether I will do something or behave in a particular way, but I do not judge others. I no longer feel rage, disdain, or anger when someone accuses me of something. I fully and completely understand why people behave the way they do and know that it is part of their struggle, their path to the light.

My life has taken on a whole new meaning, with daily rewards of peace, tranquility, joy, beauty, prosperity, and abundance. And yes, I am still a "work in progress," far, far from perfect, as Elizabeth will confirm. I have fifty-seven-plus years of ego baggage to discard and dissolve. This does not happen all at once. Patterns of thoughts and emotions that are embedded deeply in the subconscious mind and reinforced through years of repetition are like concrete. They take time, energy, daily effort, and systematic persistence to break up and dissolve. I have not mastered myself, nor have I attained complete freedom from the selfish ego-negative responses to life. My ego can still *win the round against me.* However, I now can recognize immediately when my ego is flaring up, and I ask, in that moment, for Divine assistance—and if I can be calm and open, IT comes. I am still working to rid myself of all fears, anxieties, and phobias. They continue to interfere with my peace and joy. I know I must stand up to them and use my willpower, enabling the Divine to dissolve them from my brain cells and nervous systems. It is a hurdle I am working to clear—and I know I will clear it.

I also have a seemingly persistent and chronic medical condition. I know Father-Mother-Life is working to heal it and that when the time is right, that healing will manifest in this physical plane. I don't dictate the timing. I know this: It will happen when it is right for me and right now, it is serving its purpose in driving me to continue the process of cleansing my consciousness of all rejection ego-drives. These are incremental changes, one by one; insights for the soul to learn, reinforce, and retain for all eternity.

Each of us must learn these insights for ourselves. When speaking about how, first individually and then collectively, "… *you will create the Kingdom of Heaven on Earth,"*[85] Christ tells us:

I have just one word of warning. None of this will happen until people become aware that their own human thinking only has power over the 'matter' of the world – it is not spiritual. The 'I' of each person is not the soul – the soul is hidden within the ego.[86]

Indeed, Christ tells us, your ego will remain in control of your life until you follow the process to transcend it—and open yourself to Truth:

> *Only Truth itself can open the doors, can bring insight, can bring healing. The little 'i' mind is nothing but human and finite electromagnetic consciousness, human opinions, prejudices, negative reactions, logical arguments and rationalisation born of previous experiences. Until the little 'i' of ego is able to see the Divine and open itself to receive the Divine in as great a quantity as it is prepared to give time to receiving, it will remain impervious to any Truth which may be presented to it. Indeed, it will vehemently reject it.*[87]

This opening of the ego-controlled mind to the Truth requires new knowledge, belief, faith, persistent learning, meditation, and prayer. It requires the use of willpower and it requires dedication to the goal.

Christ says that "[you must], little by little, [draw] into your minds, the transcendent Divine Consciousness to gradually spiritualise your mental processes."[88] This happens slowly, imperceptibly, and quietly, dissipating the darkness of the human ego and illuminating it with the Divine until finally your consciousness is fully illumined, and the ego is overcome. As Christ says:

> *When this happens to a person, that person becomes fully UNIVERSAL in Consciousness and is no longer aware of any desires for the self at all. It focuses on otherness entirely and lives only to experience the rapture and ecstasy of Divine Consciousness and lovingly promote the wellbeing of others.*[89]

When this happens to you, you will create little pockets of spiritual luminescence that light up your dark world. This will attract more and more people; they will be curious and will want to join you in your place of happiness.

Christ also cautions us, saying that spiritual seekers have been misled by teachers who have only understood (or only absorbed) certain aspects of his message. He explains this using the following metaphor:

> *When water is poured into porridge, it softens the porridge but it is absorbed into the porridge and takes on the consistency of the porridge. So it is when spiritual inspiration flows into a receptive mind. It takes on the nature of the human mind. Very rarely is the inspiration so powerful that...a person's beliefs are immediately changed.*[90]

Unknowingly, the teachers of whom Christ speaks teach variations of the Truth that is not consistent with the Truth and therefore they mislead spiritual seekers. Christ adds, "The fatal version is when people are told that they are Divine because they have drawn their being from Divinity."[91] This is not the Truth. "The truth is, they can draw little streams of inspired consciousness into their minds, and very little by little, the darkness of the human ego is dissipated and is illumed by Divine Inspiration. Eventually, the consciousness is fully illumined, and the ego is overcome."[92] *Beware of whom you accept as your teacher.*

Christ cautions us that:

> *If people [authors, spiritual teachers] tell you to enter into 'spiritual exercises' and 'imagine' certain conditions – be sure that if you follow these instructions, you will only keep yourself rooted in the material dimension of ego. Imagination has nothing to do with 'spirit'. Imagination is the exercise of your own human consciousness which you should be trying to transcend by entering into higher levels of spiritual consciousness.*[93]

And Christ states further: "Only [the] absolute 'Stillness' and 'Silence' of your consciousness will open the door to the entry of Divine Consciousness into your mind and that is what everyone should be seeking."[94] You can ensure you are on the right path by following the knowledge and inspiration contained within these "Letters."

This is why I stress that you read all the material yourself. It is also why, rather than providing a summary, I have included a website link in Chapter 7 to the full set of "Letters," in both .pdf and audio format.

It is of significant interest to compare the Truth of our state of being as revealed by Christ with Anita Moorjani's "experiences" of those same Truths. This comparison is important for you discern fully the difference between the Truth and the *experiential* (NDE) humanized perception of that Truth.

Now is a good time to revisit Anita's book, from Chapter 7 through Chapter 16. You will be able to comprehend, in a deeper way, Anita's descriptions of her experience against the backdrop of the Truth as described in the "Letters." Below are a few specific Truths revealed by Christ, followed by Anita's description of her experience:

LOVE

- *Christ* says that: "…irrespective of your beliefs, you are all ONE at the grass roots of your being – your souls are unified in Divine Consciousness. One and ALL, you are unified and one at soul level within your SOURCE of BEING."[95] And, he states, "The NATURE of the Divine [is] UNCONDITIONAL LOVE."[96]

- *Anita* describes the feeling she experienced as: "complete, pure, unconditional love ... unlike anything I'd known before. Unqualified and nonjudgmental…."[97]

CONSCIOUSNESS

- *Christ* says of consciousness that: "…creation is not a creation of 'matter' imbued with consciousness."[98] Rather, he says, "The universe is CONSCIOUSNESS which has taken on the appearance of 'matter' as a result of a descent into the lower frequencies of vibration of consciousness." [99] And, he says, "There is nothing in the universe that is *not* CONSCIOUSNESS made *visible*."[100]

- *Anita* describes her concept of consciousness as: "I realized that the entire universe is alive and infused with consciousness, encompassing all of life and nature. Everything belongs to an infinite Whole."[101] Her description of this Truth has been clouded over (see Christ's porridge analogy above) by the nature of her human mind. Therefore, although her experience is accurate from a *feeling perspective* as "*encompassing all of life and nature*," her humanized explanation as "*I realized that the entire universe is alive and infused with consciousness*" is consistent with our human concept of matter and consciousness and what we consider as reality.

THE FABRIC OF YOUR INDIVIDUALIZED CONSCIOUSNESS

- *Christ* states that: "Earthly Consciousness is a fabric you spin with your thoughts and feelings."[102]

- When remarking on her life and experiences, *Anita* says: "My experience was like a single thread woven through the huge and complexly colorful images of an infinite tapestry."[103] And, when referring to encounters with everyone she ever came in contact with, she states: "Every single encounter was woven together to create the fabric that was the sum of my life up to this point."[104]

FEAR

- Regarding fear, *Christ* reveals that we should: "Abandon fears, they have availed you nothing...."[105] And, he says, "By indulging your fearful thoughts, anxieties and feelings of hopelessness, you are creating the very conditions you want to rectify. You are doing all these bad things to yourselves."[106]

- *Anita* describes how fear affected her life: "My many fears and my great power had manifested as this disease."[107]

NO JUDGMENT

- *Christ* reveals to us that there is no judgment in the higher realms of spiritual consciousness: "[T]he 'Father' holds nothing, rejects nothing, condemns nothing, does not even see 'wrongdoing.' All that man does which man calls 'sin' is only of this world and is only punished within this world...."[108] And, he says, "There is no punishment from the 'Father' – whatever ills come to mankind is of their own making entirely."[109] Remember that this is a Truth, a Universal Law, the law of Cause and Effect.

- *Anita* tells us that during her NDE: "...I wasn't judged for anything.... There was only compassion, and the love was unconditional."[110]

HEALING

Anita Moorjani had a rare, transformational experience—an experience so powerful that it flashed its Truth into her awareness, causing *her beliefs to change immediately*. She was healed within days of waking from her coma.

- *Christ* reveals that to heal our bodies, we must heal our mindset: "You do not need to heal your bodies or try to make your lives better, you need to heal your beliefs!" [111] And, he says, "If you could heal your beliefs, bring your beliefs into line with the Father's true Intention for you, the wrong beliefs governing your bodies and lives would dissolve like mist in the sun."[112] Recall he further explains that, "'Sickness' is nothing more than a lowering of vitality – a reduction of LIFE – within the affected part. Restore 'Father Life' to the true Intention and Plan of your system and the entire system functions as it should."[113]

- *Anita* describes her revelation as: "I discovered that since I'd realized who I really was and understood the magnificence of my true self, if I chose to go back to life, my body would heal rapidly—not in months or weeks, but in days!"[114]

Unlike Anita, for the majority of us, healing our beliefs will be an Incremental Process; either in this lifetime or a future lifetime, depending on each individual's path and readiness.

It is likely that Anita came back for many reasons, but I believe that the primary reasons were to:

- Be living proof that if we heal our beliefs, our body heals.
- Be a witness to and record for others what happens after death: where we come from and where we return to, that we are Unconditional Love, and that we are unified and one at a soul level (within our Source of Being)—with everything!
- Testify that we are not judged after death.
- Bear witness to the fact that we are all equal, regardless of our sex, race, color, birthplace, religion, or other beliefs.
- Describe in words what she experienced (perceived) as our reality; to help us embrace the Truth described by Christ in the "Letters."

By now you have read Anita's book and the "Letters," so it is time to share with you the final steps in this seven-step process. If you have read the "Letters" in their entireties, and followed the tips outlined in Chapter 7 for doing this work, you may recognize Steps Four through Six—indeed, you may have begun the process already.

The "Letters" explain clearly that "The spiritual words of enlightenment cannot be immediately, fully comprehended by the human mind; therefore, these Letters must be read slowly and accompanied by much meditation and prayer to be properly understood."[115] Therefore, I have restated Steps Two and Three (see below) to keep all the related "Letters'" steps together and to reflect the continued work that is required to comprehend *fully* the spiritual words of enlightenment.

Step Two: Truths Unveiled.
   Required Reading: Christ Returns – Speaks His Truth (the "Letters").
   Daily Reading, Pondering, and Reflecting on the "Letters."

Step Three: Reflection.
   Required Exercise: Write Yourself a Letter.
   Do this step if you haven't yet done it as outlined in this book's Chapter Seven.

Steps Four Through Seven
   Step Four: Cleanse.
   Cleanse Your Consciousness of all Rejection Ego-Drives (and any little faults of consciousness you perceive as you grow in spiritual enlightenment). Follow the process for doing this as outlined in the "Letters."

Step Five: Re-Build.
   Re-Build Your Consciousness with Your Golden Aspirations of Divine Consciousness. If your perceptions of the highest and best evolve overtime, take your new list of your Golden Qualities back to the Divine, following the process outlined in the "Letters."

Step Six: Meditate Daily.

Meditate Daily. *"The purpose of meditation is to enable your entire consciousness to move beyond the boundaries of intellect and reason."*[116] *The "Letters" state that there is only one form of Daily Meditation that enables you to connect with Divine Consciousness. "Only through meditation will you be enabled to still and quieten your mind completely. Only then, can Divine Consciousness enter your brain cells bringing ITs own knowledge into your mind. Only then can the flaws of ego be slowly dissolved from your brain cells and nervous systems."* [117]

You must learn how to still and quieten your mind, emptying your mind completely of all thoughts. Many will claim this is impossible. But I can tell you, it is not. As I mentioned previously, mastering how to learn via listening to audio recordings helped me learn how to concentrate on the spoken word without being visually distracted. This process trained my mind to focus on the task at hand.

It takes consistent daily practice and determination to teach yourself how to do this. And once achieved, it takes additional "time for this highly spiritual experience of the Silence to become a daily routine."[118] *Learn how to do this by reading the "Letters." Memorize the Prayer (as provided in the "Letters") and keep a Spiritual Journal. If ideas, inspiration, or instructions come to you during your contact with Divine Consciousness, the moment you come out of meditation, write them down in your Spiritual Journal.*

Step Seven: Repeat.

Repeat Steps Two through Seven, skipping Step Three (as long as you have already written yourself a letter). Remember, it takes effort, persistence, determination, and dedication to achieve the goal: contact with the Divine.

My Daily Routine

I listen to audio files of the "Letters." Initially, when I started this process (at Step Two), I listened to the audio version of the "Letters" at bedtime instead of reading a book. I meditated after breakfast. This pattern changed as I grew more aware of my personal needs and what worked best for me. The following is what I settled on and it works flawlessly for me. You will have to determine what works best for you. For those of you who find it hard to fit daily meditation into their schedule, start with ten minutes, and move on to whatever timing you become comfortable with.

1. I rise naturally, without an alarm, between 4:15 a.m. and 5:00 a.m., so I can meditate before my mind is clouded or burdened by interactions with others, daily routines, or work issues. After a good night's sleep, with a waking focus on a routine of coffee, listening, then meditating, my mind is set in a clear direction and it is easier to clear my mind of thoughts.

2. I dress in comfortable clothes.

3. While I make coffee, I drink two glasses of water to ensure my brain and body are rehydrated after a night's sleep.

4. I take my coffee into my spare room and close the door.

5. I sit in my meditation chair and sip my coffee while listening for twenty to thirty minutes to a "Letter," "Article," or a "2007, 2010, or 2014 Message." I usually start at "Letter 1" and cycle through the material in order. Sometimes I only cycle through "Letter 1" to "Letter 9." Now that I have been through the material many times, I may repeat, listening to a particular "Letter" or "Message" to reinforce my learning.

6. After coffee and listening, I take a comfort break, then set my alarm on the iPad to let me know when I must rise from my meditation.

7. I put in soft foam earplugs and cover myself, feet to chest, with a favorite blanket to ensure I stay warm. I settle into a comfortable reclining position. This enables me to relax my entire body—limbs, neck, head, and face—totally.

8. I say "Good morning" to Father-Mother-Life and give heartfelt thanks for being connected to IT.

9. I thank every cell in my body for the consistent and continuous service of harmonious, loving work it does in building, maintaining, regenerating, and healing my body and for keeping me healthy and being a part of the process to help me learn the lessons I need to learn, enabling my "journeying soul to gain self-knowledge to retain individuality after it has discarded the ego."[119] I ask my body to relax, be quiet, and be still while I meditate.

10. I thank my mind for its service, acknowledging that we now know what the tools of our creativity are and that we must guard them carefully and only use them for constructive, loving purposes. I ask my mind to relax, be quiet, be still, and be free of thoughts while I meditate.

11. I say the prayer (as described and instructed in the "Letters") and settle into eliminating all thoughts. If any thought comes into my mind, I say "Father-Mother-Life" or "Divine Life." (Note: It took me many months to rid my mind totally of unwanted thoughts and allow Father-Mother-Life full scope throughout my entire consciousness system (mind, emotions, and body).)

12. My meditations typically last ninety minutes—sometimes they are shorter, sometimes longer. I have the luxury of not having to rush to work. When I started this process, my meditations were twenty to thirty minutes in length. The meditations became so wonderful, so life-giving, peaceful, and joyous that I just kept getting up earlier and earlier to enjoy a longer time with Father-Mother-Life flowing into and through me.

It will likely take many months of consistent, persistent daily effort and meditation to do this work of cleansing and re-building your consciousness and to actually "know and feel" the inflow of Father-Mother-Life. People around you (including your spouse or partner) will probably not notice many of your internal shifts and new viewpoints. Remember: One can never truly understand another person's inner state or their reality. If you persist and continue to read or listen to fifteen to thirty minutes of the "Letters" daily, followed by prayer and meditation, you will draw little streams of Divine Consciousness into your mind—and slowly but surely, you will begin to ascend in consciousness. As you penetrate the magnetic-emotional areas of the brain and new cells are impressed with new knowledge, you will feel an opening in the topmost areas of your brain, under the skull. The more you persist and progress, the larger this opening becomes. You will feel Father-Mother-Life flow into the top your head and eventually, throughout your entire body.

As the darkness of the ego fades and you become more enlightened, your soul will have greater and greater contact with Father-Mother-Life/Divine Life. Your life will change. It happens slowly, imperceptibly, until one day you wake up and realize, "I have changed!"

After you have been reading the "Letters" daily, meditating regularly, and working through Steps Two through Seven for a year or more, open the letter you wrote to yourself. You will recognize many changes in your thoughts, attitudes, beliefs, and feelings. Your outlook on life will be entirely different.

I didn't need to open my letter to realize that my depression, grief, sleeplessness, self-pity, hopelessness, and sorrow had been replaced by peace, joy, love, tranquility, and happiness. Suicide was a concept of the past. I had a new vision, a new outlook on life, and I absolutely knew my true purpose in life. I had a burning commitment and desire to be a better, kinder, and more loving and understanding person. I wanted to express every facet of the golden qualities of Divine Consciousness to everyone and everything in my environment. I cherished *every possession* I have, and my desire to acquire more *stuff* disappeared. I am happy (ecstatic really) with my life and my path to freedom. My meditations and *contact with Divine Consciousness* are my most precious, peaceful, and fulfilling time during the day.

My rhythms of "highs" and "lows" still exist, but the "lows" have become much less "low," and the duration of those "lows" have decreased significantly. I *feel* the inflow of Father-Mother-Life all day long. I can ask for Divine assistance, and IT is there, to help me, to inspire me, to protect me, and to fulfill my every need. You too can experience what I experience. You too can come out of the shades of darkness and into the light. You too can be a light to yourself and others in your orbit. As Christ says (and I echo): "I long for you to experience real happiness, real spiritual security, real fulfilment of all your needs in a way which will have no drawbacks."[120] This is Truth. This is the path I followed. Will you choose to follow it too?

This is Truth.
You too can experience what I experience.
You can come out of the shades of darkness and into the light.
You can be a light to yourself and to others.
Will you choose to follow the path to
True Spiritual Perfection?

You now possess both this *rare knowledge of self* and a process that can change the course of your life. If you believe these "Letters" are Truth (or have an inkling that they are), you are ready to begin your journey. You are now at a fork in your road. You will choose a path deliberately or by default—but the choice is up to you. Using the same logic that Elizabeth used on me when I was pondering the dilemma of taking my M.B.A., I will ask you a similar question. "If this process takes you a year (or two) to feel the peace, tranquility, joy, and Love that you long for, remember, that time will pass anyway. A year or two from now, you will look back and say to yourself either, 'I did it!' or 'I wish I had.' So, which path will you choose?" If you decide to embark on this journey, rest assured, you will not be alone—you will have Divine assistance.

In closing, I wish you well on your journey. My ardent hope for you is that you follow this path to freedom and become a beacon to others and that you choose to help initiate and create *A New Era of Love and Peace* in your personal experiences and throughout the world. And know that this book would not have been written, would not exist, without the ongoing inspiration, direction, and guidance received from the Universal, the Divine, and Christ. My gratitude is both infinite and eternal!

I cannot think of a better way to leave you than with the following excerpt from the "Letters" explaining the overall purpose of the journeying soul.

Excerpt Five:

Evolution

*There are many who will ask how it is that at the moment of conception, a soul can be drawn from **Divine Consciousness**, but the body itself may be used as a vehicle of self-expression in its coming life-span by another soul, who is ready to re-incarnate.*

When a soul is ready to enter earthly conditions on its next span of earthly learning, the soul is drawn to the parent – or parents – who can offer those conditions which will enable it to take its next necessary step forward in spiritual evolution. At the moment of conception, the old soul infuses its personal consciousness of past lives and past spiritual progress into the conception process and becomes the soul of the fertilised ovum.

Some mothers are almost immediately aware of an alien consciousness within them. The new consciousness the mother has received in her womb sometimes deeply affects the course of her thinking, her pregnancy and state of health. Once the child is born, the mother feels that she has been restored to her normal self. Sensitive mothers frequently experience an awareness of the direction their child's life will take and may think that this awareness is really born of her own wishes for her baby.

Re-incarnation is not haphazard or without a consistent plan directing its action.

The purpose is always to provide the journeying soul with many entirely different experiences which will enlarge the soul's hidden store of worldly knowledge. It provides stimulating and necessary changes of scenery and of family and environmental personalities, of characteristics drawn from genetics, but always that thin thread of the soul's journey will be buried in the subconscious mind and will surface to influence the present incarnation, although the person may be wholly unaware of it. Therefore, it is possible for characteristics, strongly held views, or passionate ambitions to be perpetuated from one incarnation to another. Sometimes the ambitions are formulated in one lifetime and only brought into a successful manifestation in the next lifetime under entirely different conditions. In such cases, before re-birth, a soul must wait until the world conditions will further the hidden ambitions of the soul successfully.

If you can imagine a soul first plunging into a red pond and coming out dyed red and entering life as a red person with all its natural red racial tendencies and educated in childhood to live 'red' lives, you will understand that the soul leaves that life with much that is red in his consciousness.

Next he will plunge into a blue pool and he will emerge blue with all the characteristics of blueness – and the lifestyle of blue people. When he leaves the world again, he will have accumulated facets of blue consciousness mixed with the red. And so it goes, life after life, the same soul growing through differing experiences of colours, religions, status, marriages, sexes, countries, politics, until finally, he wakes up to the fact that this is what is happening to him and he decides he is tired of all the various colour combinations – he wants only to ascend into LIGHT. Then his true spiritual journey starts – and gradually, by moving into one life after another, he sheds the red, blue, yellow, green, black, brown, purple accumulated in past lives, until at last, freed of all the illusions and false concepts of past lives, his soul steps out into LIGHT and re-incarnation is no longer necessary. The soul is strong, resourceful, creative – but the individuality of the soul is still inviolate and he begins to ascend into different levels of spiritual LIGHT beyond the frequencies of vibration of the world.

As I said in this Letter, I am with you always, radiating the TRUTH of BEING in consciousness. The more you read these Letters, the more you will become aware of my Presence and my Love and through this contact my loving purposes for you will be fulfilled. Only you will be able to break the contact. I am radiating Love no matter how you feel.

I leave you with my LOVE and longing for your speedy journey into Spiritual Light.[121]

AFTERWORD

My purpose in writing this book is to help as many people as possible, with the goal of creating a *New Era of Love and Peace* throughout the world. This will take many years, possibly centuries, but it starts with individuals like you. This book's success will not be measured in sales but in the number of people who read it. Therefore, if you have purchased a copy of this book, or somehow have a copy in your hands and have concluded that, "Meh ... it's not for me," or "Yes, it's the best thing since instant porridge," I urge you to pass it onto someone else (without colorful commentary on its contents) and suggest they read it. No one can judge the inner reality of another person. In order to give your friend or colleague the opportunity to decide for themselves whether the contents of this book are helpful to them, give them the chance to follow the same process you did as you read this book—without pre-judgment or external influence.

If this book can help a handful of people come out of the shades of darkness and into the light, freeing them from internal misery and pain and opening them to new experiences of peace, joy, and love, in my eyes, it will be a success. (I sincerely pray it helps many more than just a handful of people.)

Again, please help spread the knowledge and the process by passing along your copy of this book for others to read. Thank you for your help in changing the world as we know it.

—D. Neil Elliott

To learn more about the process D. Neil Elliott used for transforming his life, or to download "The Letters" blueprint document, please visit *www.AHigherRoad.com.*

If you enjoyed reading *A Higher Road – Cleanse Your Consciousness to Transcend the Ego and Ascend Spiritually*, please take a moment to review the book on your bookseller's site, or on D. Neil Elliott's website at *www.AHigherRoad.com.*

Your comments are welcomed and encouraged. Thank you.

Many blessings on your journey.
—D. Neil Elliott

APPENDIX

MY INCREDIBLE ALPINE MOTORCYCLING ADVENTURE

Because I am an enthusiastic BMW motorcyclist, Elizabeth suggested I enjoy a trip on my own. I flew nonstop, first-class on a Lufthansa Airlines round trip to Munich and spent two glorious weeks on an organized Classic Alpine tour with Beach's Motorcycle Adventures (https://www.bmca.com). The owners, Rob and Gretchen Beach, provide a first-class experience with a plethora of pre-planned daily routes to choose from. I consider them friends for life after one tour. Our group dined on first-class food and stayed in first-class hotels, with friendly and loving service all the way.

I rode most days on my own, following a pre-planned GPS route on a Garmin—and just showed up at the hotel at the end of day. The tour involves technical riding with switchbacks that have tight-turning radii (the inside turn of the pavement in some areas is no larger than a Coke can!). Some near-360-degree switchbacks had pavement that touched each way, almost overlapping around a turn. On some days, it was twenty to thirty kilometers per hour, all day long. A two-hundred-kilometer day was a long, long day. The riding required an enormous amount of mental concentration. It was exhilarating! It was the most amazing riding EVER. The views, the food, the beverages, the various cultures, and the on- and off-road experiences were unparalleled.

I can't recommend the Classic Alpine Adventure highly enough for those inclined to this type of riding—and on a BMW motorcycle of your choice to boot. Rob and Gretchen's kindness, service, hospitality, and planning with all-inclusive services make their tours about YOU and about the RIDING. Nothing else gets in your way. Your hotels, meals, options of daily routes, and luggage transfers from hotel to hotel are all taken care of by the staff of this long-standing (established in 1972) company. You are there to enjoy and have fun. They make it easy, they "make it so," and they make your motorcycle riding dreams come true, creating memories to last a lifetime. If this sounds exciting to you, contact them and ask about their tours. You won't regret it. Tell them Neil Elliott sent you!

RESOURCES

Attribution:

From the Original "Letters":

It is my, Christ's, dearest longing these LETTERS should be swiftly publicised and distributed to people seeking Truth.

Anonymous Recorder. [The online publication the Recorder titled *Christ Returns – Speaks His Truth* (aka **"CHRIST'S LETTERS"** from *CHRIST'S WAY* (https://www. christsway.co.za) (which the Recorder received from Christ between 2000 A.D. to 2014 A.D.) has been included in D. Neil Elliott's online compilation titled *A Compendium of Christ's Letters, Articles & Messages – The Path to True Spiritual Perception, Experience & Perfection: Christ's Letters – Christ Returns, Speaks His Truth.* (www. DNeilElliott. com/Resources.). [See also Endnotes 40 and 41 for source clarification —Ed.]

Begley, Sharon. *Train Your Mind, Change Your Brain.* New York: Ballantine Books, 2007. Kindle.

Brodie, Richard. *Virus of the Mind*. Carlsbad: Hay House, 2009. Kindle.

Dawkins, Richard. *The Selfish Gene, 40th Anniversary Edition*. Oxford: Oxford University Press, 2016. Print.

Doidge, Norman. *The Brain That Changes Itself*. New York: Penguin Books, 2007. Kindle.

Lipton, Bruce H. *The Biology of Belief*. Carlsbad: Hay House, 2015. Kindle.

Moorjani, Anita. *Dying to Be Me*. Carlsbad: Hay House, 2012. Kindle.

WEB RESOURCES:

(All Web Resources Accessed May 7 – 28, 2021.)

Allen, James. *As a Man Thinketh*. https://www.goodreads.com/author/quotes/8446.James_Allen.

Einstein, Albert. Albert Einstein Quotes. BrainyQuote.com. BrainyMedia Inc., 2021. https://www.brainyquote.com/quotes/albert_einstein_148819. https://www.brainyquote.com/quotes/albert_einstein_106912.

Frost, Robert. "The Road Not Taken." https://poets.org/poem/road-not-taken.

Kabat-Zinn, Jon. *Wherever You Go, There You Are*. New York: Hachette Books, 2010.

Lao-tzu. https://medium.com/@dailyzen/correcting-the-mind-1b56b0542546.

http://quodid.com/quotes/3352/lao-tzu/every-human-beings-essential-nature-is-perfect-and.

Nietzsche, Friedrich. *Friedrich Nietzsche Quotes*. BrainyMedia Inc., 2021.

https://www.brainyquote.com/quotes/friedrich_nietzsche_101616.

Shaw, George Bernard. https://www.brainyquote.com/quotes/george_bernard_shaw_386923.

Wikipedia, The Free Encyclopedia. "Richard Brodie" and "Anita Moorjani." www.wikipedia.org.

https://en.wikipedia.org/w/index.php?title=Anita_Moorjani&oldid=978621989.

https://en.wikipedia.org/w/index.php?title=Richard_Brodie_(programmer)&oldid=986405687.

URLs:

(All URLs accessed May 7 – 28, 2021.)

https://www.brainyquote.com/quotes/helen_keller_101301.

https://www.brainyquote.com/quotes/martin_luther_king_jr_101472.

https://www.brainyquote.com/quotes/ralph_waldo_emerson_101263.

https://www.brainyquote.com/quotes/thomas_merton_140834.

https://www.hayhouse.com/biology-of-belief-10-anniversary-edition-paperback.

https://www.hayhouse.com/virus-of-the-mind-3.

https://www.lexico.com/definition/belief.

https://www.ncbi.nlm.nih.gov/pmc/articles/PMC6172100/.

www.AHigherRoad.com.

www.bmca.com.

www.DNeilElliott.com.

www.lexico.com.

www.nderf.org.

SPECIAL THANKS

Special thanks goes to the Recorder from *Christ's Way*, for permission (by way of the following Attribution from the original Letters) to quote "Christ's Letters" from *Christ's Way*:

It is my, Christ's, dearest longing these LETTERS should be swiftly publicised and distributed to people seeking Truth. If quoting from my LETTERS, please state the source very clearly:

CHRIST'S LETTERS from **CHRIST'S WAY.** (https://www. christsway.co.za)

ENDNOTES

1 Robert Frost. "The Road Not Taken." https://poets.org/poem/road-not-taken.

2 Thomas Merton Quotes. BrainyQuote.com. BrainyMedia Inc., 2021. https://www.brainyquote.com/quotes/thomas_merton_140834.

3 George Bernard Shaw Quotes. BrainyQuote.com. BrainyMedia Inc., 2021. https://www.brainyquote.com/quotes/george_bernard_shaw_386923.

4 Helen Keller Quotes. BrainyQuote.com. BrainyMedia Inc., 2021. https://www.brainyquote.com/quotes/helen_keller_101301.

5 Pacific geoduck (*pronounced 'gooey-duck*) is a species of large, edible saltwater clam. —Ed.

6 Albert Einstein Quotes. BrainyQuote.com. BrainyMedia Inc., 2021. https://www.brainyquote.com/quotes/albert_einstein_148819.

7 Neville Goddard, *The Power of Awareness* (Camarillo: DeVorss Publications, 2005), 7.

8 Jon Kabat-Zinn. *Wherever You Go, There You Are* (New York: Hachette Books, 2010).

9 James Allen. *As a Man Thinketh*. https://www.goodreads.com/author/quotes/8446.James_Allen.

10 http://quodid.com/quotes/3352/lao-tzu/every-human-beings-essential-nature-is-perfect-and.

11 "The Letters," 231.

12 https://www.lexico.com/definition/mind.

13 https://www.lexico.com/definition/brain.

14 https://www.lexico.com/definition/consciousness.

15 https://www.lexico.com/definition/emotion.

16 https://www.lexico.com/definition/belief.

17 https://www.hayhouse.com/virus-of-the-mind-3.

18 Wikipedia, The Free Encyclopedia. "Richard Brodie." https://en.wikipedia.org/w/index.php?title=Richard_Brodie_(programmer)&oldid=986405687. Wikipedia notes that Richard Brodie was hired by Microsoft as their seventy-seventh employee. Brodie is known for creating the first version of Microsoft Word in less than seven months. He left Microsoft in 1994.

19 Richard Brodie. *Virus of the Mind* (Carlsbad: Hay House, 2009). Kindle.

20 Richard Dawkins. *The Selfish Gene, 40th Anniversary Edition* (Oxford University Press, 2016). Print.

21 Bruce H. Lipton. *The Biology of Belief* (Carlsbad: Hay House, 2015).

22 Lipton, *The Biology of Belief*, xiv.

23 Lipton, xv.

24 Sharon Begley. *Train Your Mind, Change Your Brain* (New York: Ballantine Books, 2007), Kindle.

25 Begley, *Train Your Mind*, 254.

26 Begley, 253.

27 Norman Doidge. *The Brain that Changes Itself – Stories of Personal Triumph from the Frontiers of Brain Science* (New York: Penguin Books, 2007), Kindle.

28 Jeffrey Long. https://www.ncbi.nlm.nih.gov/pmc/articles/PMC6172100/.

29 Ibid., 1.

30 Ibid., 8.

31 Ibid.

32 Ibid.

33 Anita Moorjani. *Dying to Be Me* (Carlsbad: Hay House, 2012), Kindle.

34 Wikipedia, The Free Encyclopedia. "Anita Moorjani." https://en.wikipedia.org/w/index.php?title=Anita_Moorjani&oldid=978621989.

35 Albert Einstein Quotes. BrainyQuote.com. BrainyMedia Inc., 2021. https://www.brainyquote.com/quotes/albert_einstein_106912.

36 "The Letters," 57. [See Notes 40 and 41 for source clarification. —Ed.]

37 "The Letters," 9. [See Notes 40 and 41. —Ed.]

38 Lao-tzu. https://medium.com/@dailyzen/correcting-the-mind-1b56b0542546.

39 Friedrich Nietzsche Quotes. BrainyQuote.com. BrainyMedia Inc., 2021. https://www.brainyquote.com/quotes/friedrich_nietzsche_101616.

40 CHRIST'S LETTERS from CHRIST'S WAY, https://www.christsway.co.za [Quotation is from the "Compendium of Christ's Letters, Articles, & Messages," 155. See source clarification at Note 41. —Ed.]

41 [As noted earlier, the Recorder called the Letters she received from Christ between 2000 – 2001 *Christ Returns – Speaks His Truth* (a.k.a. CHRIST'S LETTERS from CHRIST'S WAY at https://www.christsway.co.za). Later, between 2002 – 2014, she received a further sixteen Articles and three Messages, plus a number of other communications. While at one time you could find all of these on the various websites of the Recorder, this is no longer the case. So, for ease of reader access, I have collected these and called the compilation *A Compendium of Christ's Letters, Articles &*

Messages – The Path to True Spiritual Perception, Experience & Perfection: Christ's Letters – Christ Returns, Speaks His Truth. You can find these at *www.DNeilElliott.com/Resources.* In body text I refer to this "Compendium" as the "Letters," and in Notes I refer to the "Compendium" as "Christ's Letters." Each citation is followed by the related page number in the "Compendium." —Author.]

42 "Christ's Letters," 114.

43 Ibid., 127.

44 Ibid.

45 Ibid., 18.

46 Ibid., 293.

47 Please note that in the original "Letters," bold face font, italics, underline, all caps, centering, and other special formatting is used to emphasize particular words or phrases. Many quotes used in THIS book, drawn from the "Letters," have had most of the special formatting removed for ease of reading. To see all the words that Christ emphasized, the reader should reference the online source material at https://www.christsway.co.za.

48 "Christ's Letters," 226.

49 Ibid.

50 Ibid., 8.

51 As dictated to the Recorder, home page of https://www.christsway.co.za.

52 "Christ's Letters," 3.

53 Ibid.

54 Ibid.

55 Moorjani, *Dying,* 70.

56 "Christ's Letters," 5.

57 Ibid.

58 Ibid.

59 Ibid., 245.

60 Ibid., 1.

61 Ibid.

62 Ibid., 248.

63 Ibid., 298.

64 Ralph Waldo Emerson Quotes. BrainyQuote.com. BrainyMedia Inc., 2021. https://www.brainyquote.com/quotes/ralph_waldo_emerson_101263.

65 "Christ's Letters," 1.

66 Ibid., 131.

67 Ibid.

68 Ibid., 13.

69 Ibid., 18.

70 Ibid., 86.

71 Ibid., 119.

72 Martin Luther King, Jr. Quotes. BrainyQuote.com. BrainyMedia Inc., 2021. https://www.brainyquote.com/quotes/martin_luther_king_jr_101472.

73 "Christ's Letters," 138.

74 Ibid., 235.

75 Ibid., 301.

76 Ibid.

77 Ibid., 153.

78 Ibid., 143.

79 Ibid., 317.

80 Ibid.

81 Ibid., 235.

82 Ibid., 159.

83 Ibid., 318.

84 Ibid., 116.

85 Ibid., 317.

86 Ibid.

87 Ibid., 298.

88 Ibid., 317.

89 Ibid., 318.

90 Ibid., 317.

91 Ibid., 318.

92 Ibid.

93 Ibid., 241

94 Ibid.

95 Ibid., 93.

96 Ibid., 10.

97 Moorjani, 66.

98 "Christ's Letters," 144.

99 Ibid., 196.

100 Ibid., 129.

101 Moorjani, 70.

102 "Christ's Letters," 297.

103 Moorjani, 68.

104 Ibid.

105 "Christ's Letters," 34.

106 Ibid., 58.

107 Moorjani, 70.

108 "Christ's Letters," 47.

109 Ibid.

110 Moorjani, 108.

111 "Christ's Letters," 55.

112 Ibid.

113 Ibid., 56.

114 Moorjani, 75.

115 "Christ's Letters," 31.

116 Ibid., 219.

117 Ibid., 301.

118 Ibid., 222.

119 Ibid., 292.

120 Ibid., 278.

121 Ibid., 245.